JESSICA SWALE

Jessica Swale is an award-winning playwright and director. She trained at the Royal Central School of Speech and Drama and the University of Exeter.

Her plays include *Nell Gwynn*, which transferred to London's West End, starring Gemma Arterton, and won the 2016 Olivier Award for Best New Comedy, *Blue Stockings*, now a set text on the GCSE Drama syllabus, and *Thomas Tallis* (all for Shakespeare's Globe); *All's Will That Ends Will* (Bremer Shakespeare Company); adaptations of *Far from the Madding Crowd*, *Sense and Sensibility* (Watermill Theatre); *The Secret Garden*, *Stig of the Dump* (Grosvenor Park); radio play *Love [sic]* for BBC Radio 4 and *The Mission*, about illegal adoptions in the 1920s.

Jessica set up Red Handed Theatre Company in 2005, to develop new plays and revive classics. As Artistic Director, productions included *The Rivals* starring Celia Imrie, the London premiere of *Palace of the End* by Judith Thompson, and the first major revival of Hannah Cowley's *The Belle's Stratagem*, which won her a nomination for Best Director at the Evening Standard Awards. Red Handed won Best Ensemble at the Peter Brook Empty Space Awards 2012.

Other productions include *Bedlam* (Shakespeare's Globe); *Sleuth* (Watermill); *Fallen Angels* (Salisbury Playhouse); *Winter* (TNL, Canada); *The Busy Body*, *Someone to Watch Over Me* (Southwark) and *The School for Scandal* (Park Theatre). Jessica was Associate Director to Max Stafford-Clark at Out of Joint from 2007–2010 and has directed at drama schools including RADA, LAMDA, Guildhall, Oxford School of Drama and East 15.

Jessica is an Associate Artist with Youth Bridge Global, an international NGO which uses theatre as a tool for promoting social change in war-torn and developing nations. As such, she has lived in the Marshall Islands and in Bosnia and Herzegovina, directing Shakespeare productions including *The Comedy of Errors*, *Much Ado About Nothing*, *Twelfth Night* and *The Tempest*.

Jessica is now enjoying writing for the cinema. Current projects include *Nell Gwynn* for Working Title, *The Horrible Histories Movie* and *Summerland*, developed with BAFTA. She has written two other titles in Nick Hern Books' popular *Drama Games* series: *for Classrooms and Workshops*, and *for Devising*.

DRAMA GAMES is a series of books for teachers, workshop leaders and directors in need of new and dynamic activities when working with actors in education, workshop or rehearsal.

Also available in this series:

DRAMA GAMES FOR ACTORS
Thomasina Unsworth

DRAMA GAMES FOR CLASSROOMS AND WORKSHOPS
Jessica Swale

DRAMA GAMES FOR CLOWNING AND PHYSICAL COMEDY
Joe Dieffenbacher

DRAMA GAMES FOR EXPLORING SHAKESPEARE
Alanna Beeken

DRAMA GAMES FOR DEVISING
Jessica Swale

DRAMA GAMES FOR REHEARSALS
Jessica Swale

DRAMA GAMES FOR THOSE WHO LIKE TO SAY NO
Chris Johnston

DRAMA GAMES FOR YOUNG CHILDREN
Katherine Zachest

And more to follow…

The publisher welcomes suggestions for further titles in the series.

Jessica Swale

drama games
FOR REHEARSALS

Foreword by Marianne Elliott

NICK HERN BOOKS
London
www.nickhernbooks.co.uk

A Nick Hern Book

DRAMA GAMES
FOR REHEARSALS

First published in Great Britain in 2016
by Nick Hern Books Limited, The Glasshouse,
49a Goldhawk Road, London W12 8QP

Designed and typeset by Nick Hern Books, London
Printed and bound in Great Britain by
Ashford Colour Press, Gosport, Hampshire

A CIP catalogue record for this book
is available from the British Library

ISBN   978 1 84842 346 6

For Matt Applewhite,
the world's most patient editor,
who I'm certain never thought I'd finish
this book

'You can kill the King without a sword, and you can light the fire without a match. What needs to burn is your imagination.'

Konstantin Stanislavsky, An Actor Prepares

'All the world's a stage and most of us are desperately unrehearsed.'

Seán O'Casey

FOREWORD

The rehearsal room is a secret, mystical place where magic is meant to happen; a place where a group of terrified people come together to try to be creative, bold, imaginative, original and highly illuminating – in preparation for facing the audience that will inevitably arrive in their numbers, and judge! It is, to anybody, an overwhelming place, and, at their start, rehearsals can seem an insurmountable prospect.

But in this beautiful, and very clearly written book, Jessica Swale manages to demystify various genres of writing, unleashing all manner of meanings and depths in the text, whilst finding a way for us all to be playful. She suggests techniques to help us to break down barriers, and establish the trust amongst a company that will have to be incredibly intimate over the entire process of putting on a play.

I wish I'd had this book when I was starting out as a young director. Instinctively, I knew the great benefits of play and of games, but I had not assisted any directors that used them. I set about slowly to beg, borrow, and pinch any that I could find, writing them all out in a little notebook. To this day I still use them in rehearsals, almost every day, but particularly in the first few weeks. During rehearsals for my most recent production – at time of writing, *Rules for Living* by Sam Holcroft at the National Theatre – I shall never forget Deborah Findlay crawling along the floor, screaming, to protect her 'tail' in one game, or Stephen Mangan's brow dripping with hundreds of Post-it notes during another.

Games can be used in multifarious ways: as exercises to wake the brain up, to bind the group and give it an equanimity, to generate a sense of fun and objective, and very importantly to allow failure (without humiliation) to exist in rehearsals – because every game is about trying to achieve an objective, and every game can involve failure as well as success. The rehearsal room has to be a place where failure is allowed, is part of the process and is an instructive learning device.

But also I find games a wonderful metaphor for the text. They show how to help the actors impart the words, thoughts and concentrations of their lines. A line of text is like a ball thrown from one player to another. To throw the ball so that it may be caught requires discipline instead of sloppiness, care as opposed to laziness, and focus rather than absent-mindedness. And it demands a sense of togetherness; a sharing in the game; a sense of the whole, the ensemble.

But Jessica also finds the use of games help us to humanise Shakespeare, or Sheridan, or Wilde. She finds ways of approaching all kinds of text that has become 'stuck' or stale, during the last weeks of rehearsal – or even in performance. And she gives us tools to investigate what is beneath the written words. To help us all stop staring inanely at the text and find our own ways into it, through a sense of adventure and intrigue and fun.

I think this book will become my constant companion in future. I cannot recommend it highly enough.

Marianne Elliott
London, 2015

Marianne Elliott is an Associate Director of the National Theatre, where her productions include War Horse *(co-director)*, The Curious Incident of the Dog in the Night-time, Husbands and Sons, Angels in America, The Light Princess, Rules for Living, The Elephantom *(consultant director)*, Season's Greetings, Women Beware Women, All's Well That Ends Well, Mrs Affleck, Harper Regan, Saint Joan, Thérèse Raquin *and* Pillars of the Community. *She has also directed for the Royal Court Theatre, the Royal Shakespeare Company and the Royal Exchange Theatre, Manchester.*

CONTENTS

Part Four – SOUND AND MUSIC
In which we create the sound and sense of the world

INTRODUCTION

'Caress the detail, the divine detail.'
Vladimir Nabokov

…'That was a great show.'
  …'What a fantastic production.'
    …'That's the best performance I've ever seen.'

Every theatregoer has heard an audience gushing with praise after a particularly fine production. But what makes a 'great performance'? We can all sense when a piece of theatre moves us, or entertains us, or excites us, but have you ever asked what makes it work? There are an infinite number of contrasting ways to play a role, so it can't be about getting it 'right'. I would argue, rather, that it is about *detail*.

Good acting, in contemporary theatre at least, is most often associated with truthfulness. But what makes an actor believable? It is the detail of their performance; the rigour of their observation of real life; and their ability to recreate that on stage in a way which resonates and reminds us of ourselves. Acting is, and should be, hard work. An actor must have a profound understanding of their role and have the tools to communicate it. These skills are not only learnt through practice, but through observation of other actors.

Pick up any celebrated actor's autobiography and you'll most likely find it peppered with anecdotes about watching rehearsals; peering from the wings while they wait to enter, spying through the crack of a rehearsal-room door or saving pennies for the bus fare to Stratford to see a masterful actor at work. The one thing that all of these celebrated actors have in common is experience. Years of hard graft. They have talent, of course, too. But they've also practised. And that is something we can all do – starting now.

Most technical aspects of acting can be learnt. Voice, body and mind can all be trained. This book aims to give you the tools to do that, by providing exercises to use in your rehearsal process, which will improve and encourage a greater level of detail and complexity. Each time a company begins rehearsals for a new production, everyone has the opportunity to develop their craft. Use this opportunity both to illuminate the world of the play and present the best possible production, and to come away with skills honed for the future.

I love rehearsals. The process can be a veritable playground, an adventure in which to explore the play. It is joyful work. But it isn't just fun; it also requires diligence and precision. Without rigorous preparation in rehearsal, actors are simply guessing. And guessing leads to lack of decision-making, hazy interpretations and insecure performances which wobble from night to night like a spinning top, throwing other actors off-course. If you are a director, you can prevent all this by putting the time in to prepare your actors for their roles. And actors, you can do this work for yourself too. Know the play, the role and the context. This will make your work detailed and layered. It is this belief in the importance of rigour in rehearsals which led me to write this book.

Games in Rehearsal: How and Why

Think of the play like an iceberg. The script pokes up above the surface, but underneath there is a vast world to be mined. And not just the themes and the socio-historical context of the play; you must also understand the genre of the writing. How can you stage a Shakespeare play without understanding how verse works? How can you put on a Restoration play without knowing that the theatres were lit in a way which allowed the actors to see and speak directly to their audience members, hence the 'asides' in the text? What I hope to do in this book is to give you the tools to explore every aspect of your play, in detail, in order to find the layers and mine the text fully, both for you and for your audience.

Finding the *Play* in the Play:
My Experience of Directing *The Rivals*

I spent a good portion of my early career directing classical plays, from Shakespeare and Georgian comedies to early modern classics. One of the first was Richard Brinsley Sheridan's *The Rivals*, a Georgian comedy set in Bath, for London's Southwark Playhouse. Wondering how to prepare, I curled up with a dusty Sheridan biography and before long I was so swept up in his world that I lost all track of time. I couldn't quite believe it. This raggy old book was a revelation. This tome about the playwright's life illuminated the play in such a profound way that I felt like I'd stumbled across the 'how to direct the production' guide. The parallels between the action of the play and Sheridan's life were remarkable. He drew constantly on his own experiences. Sheridan and his protagonist were both involved in a duel for love in the fields outside Bath. Just as Lydia and Julia debate the merits of a sentimental man, so was Sheridan outraged by the frustrating fashion for sentimentalism. And as for Mrs Malaprop's obsession with learning new words, albeit incorrectly, Sheridan's father was involved in writing the first dictionary.

For the next month, Richard (we were now on first-name terms) became the main man in my life. I read the books that he read. I took myself off to Bath and spotted references to the play at every turn, pointing to details in the text I'd never considered. Mrs Malaprop amusingly (and, of course, mistakenly) compliments a character as 'the pineapple of politeness.' A funny line, yes, but it wasn't until I passed the stone pineapples adorning the grand house of Sheridan's lover that I understood the extent to which the exotic pineapple was the ultimate symbol of privilege. Malaprop's line isn't just funny, I realised, it shows her allusions of grandeur. Her faux pas is therefore doubly embarrassing as it speaks of her grappling to be seen as something she's not.

By the time we started rehearsals, not only did I feel confident in my knowledge of the text, I was eager to introduce the actors to the fascinating world I had discovered. I turned up on the Monday morning with a suitcase of photographs, Bath biscuits and vials of the pungent 'Bath water' for the actors to try. But here's the crux. We were staging a play, not writing essays. Research is all very well, but sitting and reading won't invigorate a cast. *How could I use this research in rehearsal?* And that's when I realised. *Games!* Exercises designed specifically to explore the text in a practical way. And while we're at it, why not also use games to help the actors with other challenging aspects of performance. *The Rivals* is full of long lines with multiple clauses which are hard to play. It also features asides and plenty of verbal sparring which needs great dexterity in the playing.

So, I thought, we'll use games and exercises specifically to tackle each of these challenges.

For the direct address, we played *Tea for Three*, in which the actors learned how to play to the audience – a requirement of most Restoration and Georgian comedies. To understand the specific themes of class and marriage specific to the period, we played *Pinchwife and Sons* and *Marry Your Daughters*. To help the actors tackle the long phrases we played *One-Pound Words*, to become dexterous with the complex descriptive language we played *Personal Pronouns*, and to capture the competitive sparring between Captain Absolute and Jack we played *Ha!* Theses exercises, alongside energising daily warm-ups (many of which you'll find in Part One of this book), ensured our rehearsals were demanding and dynamic. The games were never time-fillers. They allowed us to understand the play and work on the text in detail. And as we did, we began to enjoy it more and more, finding a shared love for the play and great pleasure in each other's company.

Rehearsals for *The Rivals* will always remain with me as one of the most enjoyable chapters of my working life, and, as a result of the depth with which we worked, the show went down a storm.

The joy of rehearsing is bound up in the opportunity to discover another world, a period, a place, a lifestyle… for curious nosey parkers like me, it is an ideal way to spend my time. And whilst I no longer throw my life out of the window every time I begin working on a new production, I learnt the value of contextual knowledge in understanding a text and the importance of using this knowledge in an active way in rehearsals, in order to create a layered, detailed production.

Games in New Writing Rehearsals: Nell Leyshon's *Winter*

Games can be equally helpful when rehearsing new plays. When I worked with the writer Nell Leyshon on her play *Winter*, about the lives of the early settlers in Newfoundland, the theatre company invited us to Canada to workshop the text at their coldest time of year, to give us first-hand experience of living in the arctic conditions the characters suffer in the play. Rehearsing in sallopettes, trudging the frozen roads and looking out over the icy sea gave us a glimpse of life at -30°. During the workshop period we played games every day to help the actors explore the characters and to provide Nell with context for the world she was writing about. We made *Character Graphs* to plot the development of each story over the course of the play, we played musical games like *Soundscape Orchestra* to explore the use of sound in the production, and used *The Obstacle Game* to develop the relationships between characters. By the time we returned, Nell had a brand new draft, the actors had a far deeper understanding of their characters, and I had a production mapped out, ready to go.

Why This Book?

This book is aimed at anyone who wants to explore a play. Whether you are teaching a playtext in English or Drama, leading workshops or directing a production, this book gives you tools to explore the play in a practical manner.

It provides starting points for your work, according to the specific genre of the play you are exploring. All too often we use the same approach regardless of the text, focusing simply on the story and the characters without much heed to the particularities of the writing style. A Restoration comedy requires different knowledge and skills to a modern comedy, just as playing of a Greek tragic hero makes different textual demands to portraying a Shakespearean protagonist. In this book, each genre is dealt with separately. Divided into major movements and styles in theatrical history, the exercises will help you to interrogate the context of the genre and its requirements in performance. Whilst you will find plenty of warm-ups, technique exercises and creative games here too, they were the focus of my previous two books: *Drama Games for Classrooms and Workshops* and *Drama Games for Devising*, also published by Nick Hern Books.

How to Use This Book

This book is divided into sections, from warm-ups, through character and text work, into detailed exploration of plays by style and genre, through to preparation for performance.

Part One of this book – **Getting Started** – provides exercises that can be used in any rehearsal, regardless of the type of play. Split into four sections, the focus is on warming up. Do always begin with a warm-up. It's a fantastic way to focus the group and leave the outside world at the door. It's essential to physical work, to ensure actors are ready for the demands of performance. It's also a way to practise skills that the actors will need when they begin working on the text.

This section includes both individual exercises and ensemble games to help actors prepare. The first section, *Body*, provides physical warm-ups to get the actors moving and engaging with their physicality. *Voice* is made up of both technical vocal warm-ups and singing games to help prepare for a long day's rehearsal. *Mind* focuses on tuning in, engaging and concentrating, then introduces the seeds of imaginative work. Finally, *Ensemble* provides exercises to build the company spirit.

Part Two – **The Story of the Play** – presents a series of exercises on how to approach the text. Non-genre specific, I use these games in every rehearsal process. I consider them my essential toolkit. The games help unpick a text, investigate what is said and break the play down into manageable sections. After all, a character is a character, and whether an actor is playing a comic fop or a Greek hero, they still need to know the truth of that character, to understand their objectives and to work out why they say what they say.

The main body of the book is **Part Three – The World of the Play** – which moves through theatre history period by period, providing exercises for exploring each genre. Within each chapter there are various types of activities. Some address the *style of the text*: the demands of verse in Shakespeare, for example, or the witty repartee of early modern comedy. Some address the *common characteristics of the genre*: the use of tableaux and mask in Greek theatre, for instance, or the use of asides in Restoration. Others address the *physical style* of the period: the use of the body in *Commedia dell'Arte*, for example, or the close observational style of naturalism. Finally, there are games that address *theme*. Most periods of theatre have a preoccupation with specific issues of their time: Greek tragedies often deal with hierarchy, Restoration comedies with the marriage market, and early modern comedies with life in the upper classes. These games encourage the actors to find out more about the world of the play.

The genres are divided as follows:

> *Greek Tragedy*: e.g. Sophocles, Euripides, Aeschylus
>
> *Shakespeare and His Contemporaries*: e.g. Ben Jonson, John Webster, Christopher Marlowe
>
> *Restoration and Georgian Comedy*: e.g. Aphra Behn, William Wycherley, Richard Brinsley Sheridan, Hannah Cowley
>
> *Physical Theatre and Commedia dell'Arte*: e.g. Carlo Goldoni, Molière, Steven Berkoff
>
> *Early Modern Comedy*: e.g. George Bernard Shaw, Oscar Wilde, Noël Coward
>
> *Modern Drama and Naturalism*: e.g. Henrik Ibsen, Tom Stoppard, Timberlake Wertenbaker, Caryl Churchill
>
> *New Plays*: e.g. …You tell me. They haven't been written yet.

There were many possible ways of dividing theatre history and this list is by no means exhaustive. I chose these categories because they are wide enough to cover a span of time, and most plays sit with relative ease in a certain section. There are, however, plays which fit equally in two categories, and many more which incorporate elements of several styles, and would therefore benefit in rehearsal from games from several sections. Farce, for example, can be explored through *Physical Theatre and Commedia dell'Arte* and *Early Modern Comedy*. Similarly, contemporary verse plays like Mike Bartlett's *King Charles III* or plays that experiment with lyrical form, like debbie tucker green's *born bad*, could be explored using the verse exercises detailed in *Shakespeare and His Contemporaries*.

In a sense, the more you mix sections, the more fun you can have with your rehearsal process. Be experimental. See what happens if you try the *Commedia dell'Arte* games in rehearsals for a play like Samuel Beckett's *Waiting for Godot*. It might help to release elements of the comedy. Any exercise will have value, even if it's helping an actor to realise how *not* to play a part!

In **Part Four** you will find games exploring **Sound and Music** as potential elements of your production. Music can be such an evocative layer in performance, and this section encourages you to think widely about how music and sound can accentuate the action. We also explore the use of sound effects (foley) and creative methods for composing, using the company to create soundscapes without instruments.

Finally, **Part Five** takes you up to the moment when the actors step out onto the boards, at **'Beginners'** (the call broadcast to actors before the performance begins, to let them know they must move to their starting places). This section includes games to help actors feel comfortable and confident in the space, and company warm-ups to help focus the ensemble.

A Few Final Words

Relish your rehearsal time. I love the opportunity to dive into the writer's world and discover a new period and place. And, as a playwright myself, I also love the other wonderful aspect of rehearsals: the camaraderie, which I miss when I'm stuck on my own, writing. Rehearsals offer the opportunity to embark on an exploration together, an adventure as an ensemble, and that's what makes it such a thrill. Robinson Crusoe may have had some fun on his own, but really... how much better must it have been when he had Friday to keep him company?

My motivation for writing this book is to help you make your rehearsals active, engaging and rigorous. We're all too often keen to pin the text down on day one, but there's nothing like spending a little time getting the company on to the same page, sharing research in an active manner, and enthusing them about the play you are embarking on together. With deeper insight into the world of the play, each of the actors will work with greater investment in both rehearsal and performance.

Ultimately, it is this attention to detail which will make your production come to life. Be rigorous. Work hard. And use these games and exercises to ensure your production is peopled with three-dimensional characters, telling their story in a manner that honours the world of the play and the intentions of the writer. It is the most exciting adventure to put on a play, to make theatre, and I wish you the very best of luck with it.

ACKNOWLEDGEMENTS

This book couldn't have been written without the inspiration of the many practitioners I've had the privilege to work with in the rehearsal room. Whilst each of us creates our own tracks as we head off in search of the elusive play, each path is carved with the wisdom and knowledge of those we have travelled with before.

In particular, thanks to Max Stafford-Clark, Robert Price, Francine Watson-Coleman, Lloyd Trott, Derek Bond, Adela Thomas and Kate Saxon; to the teachers who inspired me, Ron Price and Catherine Saker; and the staff and students at Exeter University's Drama Department and Central School of Speech and Drama, with whom I've played more games than you could shake a stick at.

Thank you to the team at Nick Hern Books, Matt Applewhite in particular, and to my agent, Helen Mumby at Macnaughton Lord.

You're a truly inspiring bunch.

PART ONE

GETTING STARTED

In which we warm up

Whatever the genre of play you're rehearsing, whether it's a classic comedy or a new drama, don't underestimate the value of a good warm-up. An actor has three tools to work with: body, voice and mind. Each can feel equally cold at the beginning of a long day's rehearsal. Coupled with that, if the company haven't worked together before, nerves may be running high. Either way, launching straight into Scene One won't do anyone any favours.

In this section you'll find warm-up exercises for body, voice and mind, followed by a selection of ensemble games.

Physical Games are warm-ups to energise the body and help players tune in to physicality in preparation for work.

Vocal Games begin with simple technical exercises for vocal and breath control, before moving into singing and sound games to get the vocal cords buzzing.

Focus Games are all about the mind and imagination. They are quick-thinking spontaneity games in which the actors move out of the purely physical into the realms of character and scenario.

Finally, in *Team Games* you'll find exercises to help bond the group, either through physical proximity (*Adele's Super-Hugs*) or through working together inventively (*The Boogie Pyramid* or *Top Knot*). If you're running a workshop specifically on ensemble-playing or trust, you could use these exercises to form the core of your session.

Physical Games –
Warming Up the Body

Elastoplast

A variation on classic 'It' with added physical challenges.

How to Play

Ask everyone to spread out and find a space. Choose one player to be 'It'. Like conventional 'It', the person who is up must try and tag someone by touching them. However, in this version players have a lifeline: plasters!

If someone is tagged, they can buy themselves an extra life by putting a 'plaster' (their hand) on the place where they were tagged. They then carry on playing, though they mustn't move their hand. If they get tagged again, they must use their other Elastoplast (their other hand) as a plaster, like the first. By this point they'll be running with the handicap of having both their hands attached to their 'wounds'.

When a player is tagged a third time, they must freeze and wait to be rescued. To rescue someone, two other players must come and lay a free hand on them, holding their hands on the frozen player for three counts. Then the player is 'healed' and thus free to go again. If, however, someone is tagged mid-rescue, then they become 'It' too. Game play continues until everyone is either 'It' or frozen.

The Aim of the Game

To warm up the body and create a keen sense of focus. Effective play requires observation skills and quick-thinking, so it's a good warm-up for the brain too.

Skills
Focus, Pace, Physicality

Jelly Beans

A high-speed, silly warm-up game… with almost 57 varieties.

How to Play

First, run through the following bean varieties with the group, making sure everyone knows all the beans and their associated actions:

- *Jumping Bean*: jump on the spot.
- *Runner Bean*: run around the space.
- *Jelly Bean*: wobble on the spot.
- *Baked Bean*: jumble around as if you're being cooked.
- *String Bean*: stretch to become as tall and thin as you can.
- *Broad Bean*: stretch to maximise your surface area.
- *French Bean*: take a stereotypically French pose and say 'ooh la la'.
- *Frozen Bean*: freeze. (This one is particularly useful if the game is getting a bit raucous.)
- *Has Been*: drop to the floor (or wilt, depending on how suitable it is for your cast to throw themselves on the floor).

Now, ask everyone to find a space. Then, very simply, call out bean types at random and the group must follow and behave as instructed. You might like to have music on for added beany zest. Feel free to add your own bean variations. Perhaps you could have a Pinter (Pinto) Bean variation, where everyone pauses. How about Fava Beans, Mung Beans, Refried Beans, Kidney Beans, Lima Beans… the world of pulses is your oyster.

The Aim of the Game

To warm up the group, and remove self-consciousness.

+ Recorded music
Skills
Confidence, Pace, Physicality

Running Man

A high-speed clowning warm-up to get the body and mind in gear.

How to Play

This is a part-clowning, part-physical-stamina-testing warm-up game. Everyone will need lots of energy.

Stand in a circle and play the music. Pick something with a quick tempo to get players' pulses racing. Classical music often works best because it doesn't have specific lyrics, so fits more organically with the various moods you'll be playing.

Now, everyone begins by running on the spot to the rhythm of the music, at a comfortable, enjoyable jog. Once the group have established the pace, you then throw in a new scenario and they must adapt their run to fit the situation. It's up to you whether you pause the music whilst you give your command, or speak over the top of it in order not to break the flow; it really depends how rowdy the game gets, and whether players need a breather. Here is a suggested plan. Feel free to add your own scenarios.

1. Regular run-on-the-spot.

2. A run in which you are trying desperately to snatch something (a carrot, a chocolate bar) hovering in the air in front of you, just out of reach.

3. Running away from a monster / gangster / girlfriend's angry dad.

4. Running exhausted in a marathon – then suddenly realising you're on TV.

5. Running along the beach in an American bikini commercial.

6. Running on the Moon.

7. Running in the final montage of a 'no-hoper transforms into star athlete' film in which, over the course of the run, the runner changes from a weakling to a running machine.

8. Running to deliver a letter (the participant chooses the content of the letter).

9. Crossing the finish line at the Olympic Games.

For a different style of play you might choose to play this game in slow motion. That way you can focus on the comic transitions from mood to mood, and encourage the participants to think carefully about facial expression and using their whole bodies for expression.

The Aim of the Game

To warm up the body physically and introduce elements of physical comedy.

+ Recorded music
Skills
Comedy, Pace, Physicality

Five Rhythms

A freestyle dance warm-up based on the popular '5Rhythms' movement practice.

How to Play

5Rhythms is a movement practice that was created by Gabrielle Roth in the 1970s. In its simplest form it involves the participants improvising free movement to a cycle of five different rhythms, which, between them, cover a variety of styles, dynamics and states of tension. They are danced in a cycle known as a 'wave'. The music is played and the participants are left to explore movement in response to the music, dancing entirely for themselves, on their own 'soul journey', as Roth calls it. No one is watching; this is dance for the dancer, not for an audience. Because everyone participates at the same time no one should feel like they're being watched by others.

You can use a simple short form as a warm-up, or do a longer workshop in which you allow participants about an hour to dance the whole rhythm cycle. If you choose the latter it's worth building up to it by introducing the short form in earlier sessions. Whilst at first participants are often intimidated by the notion of dancing on their own, they quickly forget about 'performing' and allow themselves to explore the movement and their bodies without paying heed to the other dancers. You might even like to schedule in a 5Rhythms session as a regular part of your rehearsal process. It's fascinating to see how a group grows in confidence and develops through repeated practice.

Begin by dimming the lights; there's nothing more self-conscious-making than bright, exposing lighting. Then play the music. Other than instructing the group to respond physically to the music, there's no reason to discuss the five rhythms. Instead, let them find their own way and, if you choose, talk about it afterwards.

Pick songs in advance which you feel encapsulate each of the following rhythms, then play them back to back. The rest is over to the dancers.

The five rhythms – and the elements they represent – are as follows:

1. *Flowing* (birth / fear / being / body) – choose soft music with a beat (e.g. 'Daniel' by Bat for Lashes, or 'Cursum Perficio' by Enya).

2. *Staccato* (childhood / anger / loving / heart) – choose faster, crisp, quick music; often pizzicato violin music (e.g. Bazzini's 'Dance of the Goblins' or Rimsky-Korsakov's 'Flight of the Bumblebee').

3. *Chaos* (puberty / sadness / knowing / mind) – choose upbeat, stirring, rowdy music, rock music perhaps, something that people can jump around to (e.g Prodigy's 'Firestarter' or House of Pain's 'Jump Around').

4. *Lyrical* (maturity / joy / seeing / soul) – choose rousing, smooth music, cool jazz or swing perhaps (e.g. Feist's '1234' or Gladys Knight & the Pips' 'Midnight Train to Georgia').

5. *Stillness* (death / compassion / healing / spirit) – choose tranquil chill-out music (e.g. Alt J's 'Matilda' or The Barr Brother's 'Static Orphans').

To find out more about 5Rhythms or to buy music created specifically for the form, visit www.5rhythms.com.

The Aim of the Game

To warm up the body and free the group of self-consciousness, whilst working with a greater sense of dynamics and states of tension.

+ Recorded music
Skills
Confidence, Physicality, Rhythm

Guess-ticulate

*A group improvisation in which players use their
physicality to reveal an idea.*

How to Play

Split the cast into two groups, A and B. A must turn
their backs. B then get into a huddle. One person
from group B chooses a word. For example, an
emotion (e.g. angry, sad) or an animal (monkey,
badger). For more experienced players choose a
state (busy, drunk, nervous), a famous person
(Winston Churchill, Marilyn Monroe) or a country
(Greece, Australia), or if you want a challenge,
choose something abstract (blue, jazz, peace, space).

Now, group A turn back round and group B must
perform their word silently; they must not use
words at all. Group A watch, then shout out their
guesses. When the correct answer is guessed, the
groups swap and whoever guessed the word right
gets to choose the next word.

For a theatre-focused alternative, you can ask the
group to choose the names of writers, genres, plays
or characters in the play you are rehearsing. It's an
excellent way to test your theatrical knowledge and
can be a fun revision tool if you are preparing for a
drama or theatre studies exam.

The Aim of the Game

To communicate ideas simply through movement
and facial expression.

Skills
Analysis, Characterisation, Imagination, Improvisation

Vocal Games –
Warming Up the Voice

Four Quick Warm-up Starters

A series of speedy technical exercises to get everyone's voices warmed up before launching into rehearsals.

How to Play

Ask the players to stand in a circle. Take them through each of the exercises below, demonstrating each instruction as you give it, so that they can copy you. Repeat each of these exercises several times, using a little more voice each time.

The Yawn

Do an exaggerated yawn. Open your mouth as wide as you can. Now, as you yawn, begin making a high sound, at the top of your register, and point your finger up in the air above your head. Now, as you let the air out, gradually drop your tone lower and lower, and trace the journey with your finger, from high to low, until you finish pointing at the floor with your voice as low as you can go. This exercise will stretch the back of your throat, opening your vocal cords. Repeat a few times, making sure you breathe properly in order to support your voice. Each time you repeat it, use a little more voice to produce a fuller sound.

Tossing the Ball

Pick up an imaginary ball from the floor in front of you. Pull it back behind your head as if it was a ball that you are about to throw. As you pull it back, make an 'ee' sound, as if gearing up for the big release. Then throw the imaginary ball forward on a 'yaah' sound, releasing your jaw to allow the sound to swell. Use forward projection to push the sound away from you, and continue the sound until you run out of breath and the 'ball' has landed.

Brushing Your Teeth

An exercise for the tongue. Tongue articulation is an essential part of vocal clarity. Do the following sequence to give your tongue a quick warm-up:

- Stick it out and roll it back in.
- Stick it out and move it north, south, west and east (up, down and side to side).

- Place it in the bottom of your mouth then flick it into the roof. Pull it back as far as you can retract it, then press it against your teeth.

- Use it as a toothbrush and see if you can move it all around your teeth, touching all of them on its journey, front and back.

- Finish with a few kisses and smiles: tightly kiss your lips together, then smile broadly.

Mouse and Lion

Squish your face up into the smallest tiniest little mouse face, screwing up your features and closing the eyes tight. Then release and make the widest face you possibly can, the lion face, sticking out your tongue, extending your eyes and cheeks and giving a great exhalation of breath to sound like a 'rah' sound. Repeat this, shifting quickly from your tiny mouse face to the extended lion.

The Aim of the Game

These four simple exercises are all easy ways to begin your vocal warm-up, encouraging the participants to begin exploring their voices, employing projection, using the tongue and opening the vocal cords.

Skills
Voice

Tongue Twisters

A series of quick-fire tongue twisters to improve articulation.

How to Play

Try these tongue twisters. You can use them in rounds, put them into a sequence or pick or choose to use them however you see fit. Either do them in a circle, so participants can see each other, or, once players know them well, try pacing round the room. Repeat each four or so times, beginning in a whisper and moving to full voice. Whispering a phrase clarifies the consonants, so it's a good way to get everyone's mouth muscles working.

- To titillate your taste buds, try these tasty titbits.
- Seventy-seven benevolent elephants.
- Really rural.
- Fresh fried fish, fish fresh fried, fried fish fresh, fresh fish fried.
- Worldwide web.
- How can a clam cram in a clean cream can?
- Willy's real rear wheel.
- Pirate's private property

The Aim of the Game

To warm up the vocal muscles and focus on articulation.

Skills
Articulation, Clarity, Physicality, Voice

Rhythm Ball

An exercise in which each voice adds to the ensemble to form a rhythm choir.

How to Play

Stand in a circle. One person, Player 1, has the ball. Player 1 begins a vocal rhythm, a short phrase of vocal sounds with strong beats (ideally in 4/4 time, i.e. over four counts), which can easily be copied and sustained. They repeat it a couple of times, then throw the ball to someone new (Player 2). Player 2 must join in with Player 1's rhythm for two full repeats, before changing it to something new, which complements the original phrase. Meanwhile, Player 1 continues with their original phrase.

Player 2 then throws the ball somewhere else – to Player 3, who similarly, repeats Player 2's phrase for two rounds then makes a new one up, before throwing the ball on to Player 4, etc. Each player continues with the rhythm they invented, so by the time the ball has been passed round the whole circle, you should have a complete orchestral score of different rhythms in this circular beatboxing extravaganza.

The Aim of the Game

To build a sound picture as an ensemble, to boost listening skills and to start being creative with rhythm and musicality.

+ A ball
Skills
Ensemble Work, Listening, Rhythm, Voice

Lip Tips and Tongue Ticklers

Exercises to get your mouth working.

How to Play

Loosening both the tongue and the lips is critical for clarity of speech. Certain consonants use the lips, plosive sounds like 'P' and 'B', for example. Try it, you can feel the contraction and roll of your lips actively working to producing the popping sound. Others require the tongue to be much more active, like a 'T' or a 'G' sound; feel how your tongue moves in the mouth to produce these different sounds. Here are a couple of simple exercises for the lips and tongue to help everyone activate those muscle groups.

For the lips:

Firstly, ask the group to speak each of these lip-based consonants and observe how the shape of their lips changes as they do so.

> Baa maa paa
>
> Waa vaa faa
>
> Zaa shaa chaa

Now speak them in a rhythm running through different vowel sounds. Stand in a circle and speak them to a beat. Ask the group to tap their feet to sustain momentum.

> Bee bay bah boh boo
>
> Mee may mah moh moo
>
> Pee pay pah poh poo
>
> Wee way wah woh woo
>
> Vee vay vah voh voo
>
> Fee fay fah foh foo
>
> Zee zay zah zoh zoo
>
> She shay shah shoh shoo
>
> Chee chay chah choh choo

For the tongue:

Now ask the players to speak each of these tongue-loosening consonants, paying attention to the placement of the tongue for each.

> Daa taa gaa caa zaa saa.

Now, speak them in rhythm in your group.

Dee day dah doh doo

Tee tay tah toh too

Gee gay gah goh goo

Cee cay cah coh coo

See say sah soh soo

Follow them with some phrases that use the same oral shapes. Speak each several times, emphasising the lip and tongue movements to help clarify the sound and warm up the muscles.

- Tip-top tippy toes,
  Chip shop, chippy cheese.

- Gurgling curs, gargling cars

- Did you, would you,
  Could you, should you?

- She saw see-saws

You can easily make some of your own using the sounds listed here or ask the group to invent some.

The Aim of the Game

To warm up the lips and the tongue fully.

Skills
Articulation, Clarity, Voice

Shakespeare: The Musical!

A singing exercise to free the text and warm up the voice.

How to Play

One of the best ways to warm up the voice is to sing; it encourages us to use our full pitch range and to employ a variety of tone types and dynamics. It also requires us to use our 'head' and 'chest' voices and to breathe more consciously to support our voices. So what better way of preparing to speak the text than by singing it?

Begin by choosing the singing style for your piece. Choose something that relates to the genre of the scene: a more emotional dramatic scenario might warrant an operatic style, rather than a pacey comedy, which might be best sung as a patter song in the style of Gilbert and Sullivan's 'Modern Major General' from *The Pirates of Penzance*. Try these for size:

- *Gilbert and Sullivan operetta.*
- *Hip-hop musical.*
- *Folk song or ballad.*
- *Country and western.*
- *Rock opera* (though be careful not to strain the voice).
- *High opera.*
- *Barbershop quartet.*

Now, stand in a circle. Each time a character enters the scene, the actor must jump into the circle and sing all of their lines, making up an appropriate tune in the style you've selected. Each actor remains 'in the ring' until their exit. It really is as simple as that.

As much as this game seems like just a bit of fun, it's a fantastic means of uncovering the specific rhythms, sounds and cadences in the text. Alliteration (words that begin with the same letter, e.g. pink pigs) will be easier to identify; rhymes and assonance (words that contain the same vowel sound, e.g. fast cars) are often more audible in singing than in reading aloud. Use of pause becomes specific and playful, and, if your play is in verse, then the rhythm will jump straight to the fore. Everyone needs to pay attention to these elements as they are both singing and listening.

It's preferable to play this game at a point when the cast know their lines so they can work with a greater sense of freedom, but there's no reason why you can't play with scripts in hand if you choose.

The Aim of the Game

To warm up the voice and draw attention to the text's rhythm and language.

+ **Your scripts**
Skills
Articulation, Breath, Imagination, Voice

Broadway Baby

A comic singing warm-up to play in teams.

How to Play

Put a chair in the space and ask an actor to sit on it. This lucky person is going to be serenaded by a pair of Broadway stars.

Select two players from the group. Tell them that they are the most confident, talented musical-theatre writers that the world has ever known… and they are going to improvise a song together, especially for their guest.

Begin by asking the guest to state what subject they would like to be serenaded about. It could be anything from a part of their body (their left toe, for example), an object or theme they particularly desire (e.g. banana custard, the state of the economy, corkscrews, spider monkeys, sea slugs – the more random and specific, the better).

The singing pair must now improvise a Broadway-style song on the given theme. Encourage them to end it with all the gusto of a huge Broadway number. If you want to make it even harder, limit them to singing it one word at a time, passing the 'baton' from player to player.

If you want to involve more participants, then replace the two Broadway stars with a Broadway choir. I'd advise no more than four singers though, as part of the joy is working together as a team and having to jump in in such quick succession.

In order to allay the fears of less musical participants, make it clear that the aim isn't to sing brilliantly – it's to be creative, have fun and to be confident in your choices. And it doesn't have to rhyme, it just has to engage the audience.

The Aim of the Game

To warm up the voice and encourage imagination and confidence.

Skills
Articulation, Breath, Imagination, Improvisation, Voice

Focus Games –
Warming Up the Mind

Word Pong

A quick-fire word-association game. Think 'It' but with words!

How to Play

Everyone stands in a circle.

Now, choose which version of the game you would like to play. In the simple version, the group riffs on a single theme. You give a word as the 'starter word'. Then, round the circle, in quick succession, each player must say a word associated with the starter word. For example, if the starter word is 'paper', players can name any word related to that original word, e.g. wood, news, printer, recycled, tree, etc.

Alternatively, for a more challenging game, players must say a word associated with the last word spoken, so that the game that starts on one theme will rapidly move somewhere different. For example, to use the same starter word ('paper'), the game might play out like this: paper – aeroplane – flight – bird – penguin – book – worm – mud – forest – Amazon – river, etc.

The idea is to keep the rhythm of the game going, so there must be no hesitation. If you choose you can give players three lives and, if they hesitate three times, they are out. As player numbers dwindle, the game inevitably culminates in a head to head between two finalists.

If you want to add an extra layer, you can allow players to gain a point if they can get back to the original word.

You can also play this game in pairs. The two-player version is a good way to build relationships between company members, whereas the ensemble version can be used to find a sense of group focus.

The Aim of the Game

To focus the group and to encourage the players to think quickly and spontaneously.

Skills
Focus, Improvisation, Vocabulary

Ring of Masons

A movement game in which a player has to spot the secret leader.

How to Play

Everyone stands in a circle. One player is sent out of the room. That player will become the inspector, whilst the rest of the players become a secret society.

Everyone else decides on a leader for the society, who, like in any secret organisation, must remain anonymous to the outside world. It's the group's collective responsibility to ensure they are not found out. Invite the inspector back in. Now, whatever the leader does, the rest of the group must copy, simultaneously, but all the time trying to move as one, so that the inspector cannot work out who the leader is. The members of the secret society should begin with slow subtle movements, though as the leader gains confidence and observes the dynamic of the group, they might try throwing in some bolder, rapid movements to test the inspector's wits.

The inspector gets three guesses. When they have guessed (or used up all three guesses and been told), then the secret leader becomes the inspector, and the game begins again.

The Aim of the Game

To encourage the cast to act as one with focus and precision.

Skills
Ensemble Work, Focus, Observation

Alphabexercise

A speedy improvisation game using alphabetical order.

How to Play

You can either play this game with one pair and the rest of the ensemble watching, or ask the whole company to play simultaneously.

Give the pair(s) a scene title. It can be something straightforward, 'Jane and Mo Go to the Zoo', or something deliberately intriguing: 'The Secret' or 'The Unexpected,' for example.

Now, there is only one rule, but it's a tough one. The actors must speak each new line beginning with the next letter of the alphabet. To take our zoo scenario, for example, the improvisation might go something like this:

> JANE: All the monkeys in this cage have blue bums!
>
> MO: Bet you'd have a blue bum if you were stuck in there after living in the jungle for most of your life.
>
> JANE: Can't be right, them being caged up like this.
>
> MO: Don't suppose you'd be up for helping one escape?
>
> JANE: Escape!
>
> MO: Follow me – I've got some wire-cutters in my bag…
>
> JANE: Get them!

And so on.

The easiest way to play is alternating speakers so you only give one line each. However, you can play with a 'free for all' rule, where an actor can carry on speaking as long as they continue to alphabeticise at the start of each sentence. A quick-thinking actor might say something like: 'Can you believe it? Didn't think it was possible. Everybody said I couldn't do it. Fools, the lot of them.'

The only rule is stick to the alphabet. You might find there are rather odd pauses at certain points, most often around Q and X! It's also best to avoid exclamations at the beginning of each sentence. It's tempting to say 'Blimey, look at that!' 'Cor, I've never seen anything like it.' But in truth that's a bit of a cheat as the real action of the sentence doesn't begin with the exclamation. Instead, encourage players to speak in whole, single-clause sentences.

Variation

For an alternative version of this game, rather than limiting the actors to letters of the alphabet, play with the rule that they can only ask questions. As soon as one person makes a statement, they drop out and another actor runs in. Give it a go, it's harder than it sounds!

The Aim of the Game

To focus the mind and to build up an ability to think quickly whilst in character.

Skills
Focus, Improvisation

Chair Pairs

The quickest and most literal 'sit'-com of all time.

How to Play

One player sits on a chair in the space. Everyone else forms a line at the side of the room, waiting with their chair. The first player begins a solo improvisation, they could be waiting in the airport lounge, an interview candidate, Humpty Dumpty sitting on his wall, whatever they like. Now, when the next person in line sees an opportunity, they run in with their chair, sit down on it next to the original actor and begin a new scenario, now with two chairs. They could be two builders having their lunch, two nervous swimmers waiting to jump into a pool, two gnomes fishing. The incoming actor must make the new scenario clear as he or she sits down so that the first actor knows how to participate. Now, the chair pairs have begun.

As soon as the next person in line is ready, they swoop in with their chair, which boots the first actor out, who must leave with his or her chair, meaning that there are always a pair of chairs in play. The game is to see how many different scenarios can be found within this limitation.

You can choose to allow the configuration of the chairs to change, so they are one in front of the other, facing each other, back to back or however the player chooses. But in some ways the simplest arrangement (chairs next to each other) is the best because it forces players to be creative within the limitations, and therefore makes for more imaginative results.

The Aim of the Game

To think on your feet (or, rather, on your seat) in order to create quick, fully realised scenarios, and to practise responding openly to new ideas without 'blocking' them.

+ Same number of chairs as players
Skills
Ensemble Work, Imagination, Improvisation, Pace

Plasti-Scene

A version of 'Freeze!' in which players mould each other into new improvisations.

How to Play

Everyone stands in a circle. Choose one player to be 'up'. They must take the floor and begin a solo improvisation. They could be doing anything: wandering around a botanical garden, for example, or composing a symphony. Now, at some point, a player in the circle can shout 'Freeze!', causing the first actor to freeze. The new player then enters the space and moves the original player round into a new position, as if they were made of putty, and then brings this scene to life by speaking a line, which unfreezes the first player and kick-starts the new scene. For example, having moved the actor into a birthing position and taken a position facing them, the player entering the space might begin the new scene by shouting: 'It's coming, I can see the head! Push!'

For the simplest version of the game, each time someone shouts 'Freeze!', the new entrant replaces the player who has been in the longest, so the game remains a two-player game, with each participant having a chance both to initiate and respond to a scene.

Variation

To involve more players, you can play a version where the new player adds themselves into the scene, rather than replacing another player, so that the game gets bigger each round. If you choose to play like this, you can specify whether the new player must manipulate all the frozen characters into a new scene, or just one key character.

The Aim of the Game

To free the imagination and encourage spontaneity.

Skills
Characterisation, Imagination, Improvisation

Up in Arms

A very silly mime game for pairs.

How to Play

Set out two chairs and nominate two actors, A and B, to sit in them with their arms behind their backs. Now allocate two more actors (C and D) to be their arms. The 'arm' actors must kneel behind the chairs, slip their arms through the sitters' arms and act as their hands.

Ask the rest of the group to suggest a subject matter to be the topic of an interview, which gives the actors their characters: e.g. an astronaut's first space-walk or an scientist's discovery of an invisibility potion. A is the interviewer and B the expert interviewee, who will talk in detail on the subject. As they talk, C and D will gesticulate for them. Obviously, the more emotional or dramatic the interview becomes, the more fun the 'arm' actors can have with their gesticulations. Similarly, if the subject matter is something technical or physically interesting, there may be comic mileage in getting the expert to demonstrate.

Good improvisers will purposefully make life difficult for each other by asking challenging questions or setting each other up. The results can be hilarious.

The Aim of the Game

To encourage the pairs to work as a team to create one coordinated character, and to hone improvisation and comedy skills along the way.

Skills

Characterisation, Communication, Ensemble Work, Improvisation

---

Team Games – Creating an Ensemble

To Be or Not to Bee

A free-style group-improvisation game.

How to Play

This game is the very simplest in form and one of the most fun to both watch and participate in. Split the group into two. One half finds a space in the room, the other half sits against the wall as the audience. Put on some jaunty, upbeat music that's easy to listen to, to serve as background music for the game. Jazz standards like Nina Simone's 'My Baby Just Cares for Me' or Billie Holiday's 'The Very Thought of You' are ideal.

Now, the audience members shout out words that the players have to respond to immediately, in whatever way first comes into their heads. Instructive words are straightforward: 'bounce', 'walk', 'run', 'freeze'. But as the game goes on, the audience will undoubtedly think of more abstract words: 'city', 'love', 'hunger', 'pink'. The most interesting words are those with multiple meanings. If the word is 'be', for example, some of the players may just lope around, being in the space, or stand still. Others may begin buzzing, having taken 'be' to mean 'bee'.

Ask the audience to observe carefully and see what they find interesting. It's often engaging to look at how, at points, players may interact with each other, finding characters, making narratives, which they may sustain for a few words, before moving on. It can be surprisingly beautiful to watch.

After a song or two, swap over so that the audience become the players and vice versa. Encourage the players not to repeat any of the words used in the first round.

The Aim of the Game

To encourage actors to engage spontaneously with the material, and to trust their instincts.

+ Recorded music
Skills
Communication, Ensemble Work, Physicality

Adele's Super-Hugs

Possibly the friendliest of all warm-up games.

How to Play

This is director Adele Thomas's favourite game, and it's a great way of jumping in at the deep end with a new company.

Ask the players to find a space in the room and choose someone to be 'It'. Like conventional 'It', that person's job is to tag people by touching them. However, they are only allowed to move by putting one foot in front of the other, touching heel to toe, so they are restricted from moving too fast. Everyone else can move as fast as they wish.

Sounds quite like conventional 'It' so far, doesn't it? But here's the difference. In this version you can protect each other by hugging. So, if you see someone about to be tagged, you can hug them and, whilst you are in an embrace, you are both safe. However, when someone does get tagged, they become 'It' too, so there's an ever-increasing number of taggers. So in order to play effectively, get hugging. Just be sure you don't accidentally hug a tagger!

While many groups of actors will feel perfectly comfortably hugging each other, do consider the make-up of your group before choosing to play this game. It may not be appropriate, particularly if you are working with vulnerable groups.

The Aim of the Game

To warm up physically whilst creating a physical ease between everyone in the cast.

Skills
Ensemble Work, Focus

Top Knot

A detangling game to get the group to work together efficiently.

How to Play

Everyone stands in a circle and begins by putting their left hand in and taking one other person's hand. Then, everyone puts their right hand in and finds someone else's right hand to hold. From this point on, no one is allowed to break hold.

Now, with any luck, the players will be tied in an enormous human knot. The idea is for the group to unknot themselves without releasing hands. They may well find they are actually in two circles – or more! Or that some players end up facing the outside of the circle and others inwards.

The group need to be patient and work carefully to unknot themselves. It may only be possible for one person to move at a time. They'll quickly find that, if everyone tries to unknot themselves at once, they'll have a disaster on their hands. Instead, if you encourage the group to work as a team and listen to one another, the problem will be much easier to solve.

The Aim of the Game

To use teamwork to untangle the knot in the most efficient way, encouraging the players to collaborate effectively.

Skills
Ensemble Work, Physicality

Falling Trees

An ensemble trust game.

How to Play

All the players walk around the room, moving into available spaces as they go. At any point a player can shout: 'I'm falling.' They must speak clearly and loudly to ensure they are heard. They then begin to fall. They must do this safely. In order be caught easily, they must fall backwards, rolling back on their heels and then falling towards the floor rigidly, keeping their back straight and their arms tucked in by their sides. It is imperative that they fall towards the centre of the room, so that everyone else can predict from a distance which way they are going to fall. As soon as they begin to fall, the ensemble near them must swoop in and gently catch them, supporting their weight and lowering them down until they are lying flat on the floor. They can then get up and game play resumes.

Be careful when playing this game. You must make sure that the speakers are clear when they call out 'I'm falling', as if they aren't heard, they'll end up on the floor. As soon as one person begins to fall, no one else can fall. It's imperative to make sure no one is in danger. It takes some nerves to fall, but as the game progresses and players witness the safety with which each person is caught, even nervous players usually gain the confidence to try it.

It should go without saying that pregnant women, small children or players with injuries or bad backs should not play this game. Also you might like to limit the playing space if you're in a massive sports hall, in order to ensure no one falls at such a distance from other players that they can't be reached in time!

The Aim of the Game

To build a sense of trust within the ensemble.

Skills
Focus, Pace

The Boogie Pyramid

An improvisational dance game.

How to Play

Any music will do for this game, but upbeat, joyful music which gets people moving is the best, e.g. Pharrell Williams' 'Happy' or Aretha Franklin's 'Respect'.

The group starts by standing in a triangle formation, with one person at the front of the pyramid, two behind them, three behind them, etc. As you run out of people, keep the edges of the triangle intact, just have fewer people in the line.

Play the music. The person at the front begins to dance. The row behind them must copy, but add 20% to the scale of the movements. The line behind copy the line in front, but add 20% in scale, continuing back until the people at the very back are doing crazy dancing.

Play like this for a little while, then add a further challenge with the following instructions. Call out:

'Switch left!': The group must all rotate on the spot, to the left until they are facing the back left-hand corner of the triangle, which becomes the new front. The person who was stationed on that corner now becomes the leader.

'Switch right!': The group all swivel right, until the back right-hand corner of the triangle is the new front, and the person at that corner the leader.

'Chain!': The players move in and out of each other in their lines, moving along the lines passing each other, switching positions as they go, until you shout: 'Stop!' This is the new configuration of the line.

'Free fall!': Everyone dances off in their own directions until you shout: 'Reform!', at which point they dance back into new places, making sure they are in a different line and position, thus mixing up the pyramid.

'*Back to the front*': The leader must dance to the back and swap with someone of their choice from the back row, who dances to the front and becomes the new leader.

In order to keep the triangle, you might like to mark it out in chalk or tape on the floor, so that it's easier to reform when the group continues to move.

Variation

In order to link this game to your play, you might like to choose appropriate music. If you are rehearsing a play set in the eighties, for example, choose an artist like Spandau Ballet or Queen, and get the group to dance along using their best retro moves. If you want to go further, it's always fun to encourage them to play in character.

The Aim of the Game

To warm up physically, to increase the group's level of ease with each other and to have a good old boogie.

+ Recorded music
Skills
Ensemble Work, Focus, Physicality, Rhythm

PART TWO

THE STORY OF THE PLAY

In which we get to know the text

'Words are sacred. They deserve respect. If you get the right ones, in the right order, you can nudge the world a little.'

Tom Stoppard, The Real Thing

'He liked all books because he liked the mere act of reading, the magic of turning scratches on the page into words inside his head.'

John Green, The Abundance of Katherines

So the company has warmed up, they are physically energised, their vocal cords are humming, they've never felt more focused – and they can't wait to get started on the play.

Ah yes, the play.

Pages and pages of words that must be magically transformed from these 'scratches on the page' into a rich and layered performance. How? Good question.

The French for rehearsal is *répétition,* but there's very little value in simply repeating and regurgitating. All too often rehearsals are seen as the period in which actors repeat scenes, over and over again, adding to them a little each time like layers of oil on a canvas until they have painted a complete picture. With each repetition, the actors may become more familiar with the lines, fix where to stand, rerun the same emotions with a little more confidence until they have a perfectly adequate 'well rehearsed' performance... but where's the *play* in that? Where's the exploration? Where are the opportunities to shift gear, to try something, to unravel? In order to play a character, an actor must explore the person they aim to become, interrogate who they are and ask why they do what they do. By asking questions, an actor can seek out the best interpretation of a role, rather than the first interpretation they come upon. They will find detail.

Use rehearsal time to investigate the text fully. Don't just chew the cud, explore. Unpick the phrases, consider how characters speak, what they say both in the literal sense and in subtext. Look at what's not being said. Consider specific choices of language and what that implies about them. Writers of good plays are grafters; you can bet that every sentence you speak has been pored over, reworked, considered down to very last syllable. So if the writer has put that much time into getting your line right, so should you.

In this section, each of the exercises provide practical tools for unpicking the text. They are weapons against fast-food interpretation. They force the entire company to listen, to interrogate and to think. Some are good for early points in rehearsal, when you are considering the text for the first time. Others suit the later stages, where everyone has become so familiar with the lines that they require new ways to look at them. Enjoy these games, adapt them, try them all out and see what surprises rise to the top of your textual broth.

In *The Listeners* we focus on the characters' motivations for speaking, whilst in *One-Pound Words* we look at how to clarify the specific meaning of the text through careful intonation. *Personal Pronouns* moves the focus to the characters' vocabulary in an active exploration of the use of nouns, verb and adjectives. In *Jazzercise* the actors have the chance to play with rhythm and pause to keep the other speakers on their toes. *The Obstacle Game* provides a series of tools to ease the pressure off an obsession with 'getting the text right', to find freedom when you are stuck in a pattern or a rut. In *Shadow Play* the actors are fed the lines so they can work without scripts in hand. Finally, *The Rubber Duck of Doom*, which is as silly as its name suggests, encourages actors to work outside the emotional trajectories they have decided on, by throwing others into the mix.

I regularly use these games in my rehearsal process.

Some have become absolute essentials. I use *One-Pound Words*, *Personal Pronouns* and *The Listeners* in every production process without fail. They are fantastic for easing the company into the text and encouraging the actors to explore without the pressure of giving a performance too early. Plus, there's always one scene in the play that causes problems, and all too soon becomes *the scene of doom* that everyone is fearful of. When you work out which scene that is, throw in one of these games from left-field. Often it'll be just the release you need to find something new in the scene that the actors can feed off and enjoy.

The Listeners

23

A game in which players work out what sparks their thought.

How to Play

This is one of my all-time favourite rehearsal exercises; I find it invaluable. It is one of the simplest exercises in this book, but one of the best.

It is easy for actors to fall into the trap of focusing so much on their own lines that they forget to listen fully to their scene partners. By encouraging them to listen and to pick up exactly what gives them the idea for their line from the other person's dialogue, they can find closer connection and greater spontaneity in their performance.

Ask the actors to play the scene. They must play it once through normally and ask them to focus specifically on listening to each other. Now, play it again, but this time ask the actors to repeat the end of the previous speaker's line at the beginning of theirs, in order to pinpoint the fragment that has spurred their response. It is most often the end of the other speaker's line – or a part thereof – but it may well be something earlier in that character's speech.

Let the actors choose freely, and work spontaneously as they play the scene out. It is easier to do the exercise with scripts, even if they know their parts, in order to allow them to articulate the other person's lines easily. They may need to change pronouns and rephrase statements as questions in order to state the line as if it is their own. This is fine, and to be encouraged.

Let's take a scene from *As You Like It* as an example. The italic text is an example of what the two actors vocalise from the preceding line to show what prompts their response:

ROSALIND: Do you hear, Forester?

ORLANDO: *Do I hear?* Very well: what would you?

ROSALIND: *What would I?* I pray you, what is't o'clock?

ORLANDO: *What o'clock?* You should ask me what time o'day: there's no clock in the forest.

ROSALIND: *No clock in the forest?!* Then there is no true lover in the forest, else sighing every minute and groaning every hour would detect the lazy foot of Time as well as a clock.

ORLANDO: *As well as a clock?* And why not the swift foot of Time? Had not that been as proper?

ROSALIND: *The swift foot of Time? Had not that been as proper?!* By no means, Sir. [Etc.]

You can use this exercise in early sessions to help investigate a scene for the first time, or as a way to find fresh life in well-rehearsed scenes if you find the actors are stuck in a rut.

The Aim of the Game

To clarify thought and pinpoint the motivation for speaking. So often the problem in a scene can be that the actors are concentrating on acting rather than reacting. This game nips that in the bud, and the resulting improvement can be dramatic.

Skills
Listening, Observation, Spontaneity

24 One-Pound Words

This is voice genius Robert Price's wonderful exercise for the prevention of overdramatising.

How to Play

If you ever listen to radio drama you can hear the difference between clear radio acting, where actors pick one or two words in a sentence to emphasise, and bad radio acting in which, in order to be dramatic, EVEry WORD is GIVEN HUGE IMPORtance so that we HARDly KNOW what the FOCUS of the LINE is. It's a real problem, and this overstressing bad habit means that, whilst a scene can seem dramatic, it's almost impossible for an audience to figure out what the character thinks, feels and means.

It's particularly problematic in period texts. In auditions for Restoration comedies in particular, actors often dramatise all the florid language, giving wonderfully exuberant performances, but leaving us non-plussed about the meaning of the lines.

The truth is that we only usually stress one or two words in normal speech patterns. This helps the listener to identify the focus and meaning of a sentence, and through it, the speaker's objective. Listen next time you are on the bus. It's true the world over.

All good voice teachers teach the importance of finding the 'nub' of the line, the 'keyword' – whether they call it the 'hot word', the 'nucleus of the line' or something else. My favourite, though, is Robert Price's method. Robert teaches us to look for the 'pound word', suggesting that the rest of the sentence should, comparatively, be worth pennies. I find this most useful because not only does it help the actor to focus on a keyword, but it encourages them to let the rest of the sentence go. That doesn't mean drop it completely – it should still be clear and interesting, but you only have a little money to spend – so it's one pound only, not an abundance of scattered silver.

Ask the actors to go through their scripts with their scene partner(s) and work out what the keyword is in each line (or, in lines of immense length, within in each clause or thought). Try it various ways. Sometimes there's an obvious keyword; sometimes it's hard to choose; sometimes it is something quite surprising. If in doubt, verbs are often the most interesting choices. Now ask the group to read the scene and play their underlined words at the value of a pound, and everything else to the comparative value of a penny. Be strict – no ten or twenty pences – you are on a tight budget. It is incredible how much clearer a speech becomes when a lot of the emphasis is taken away. Beckett was right. Less is more.

If your text is verse, try this exercise ignoring the demands of the verse, i.e. if you are using iambic pentameter, then speak it as if it is normal text, and only emphasise one word in a line as the game dictates. Then layer the rhythm back in lightly, still allowing your chosen word to be the strongest. You will find in almost every case that your emphasised word is on one of Shakespeare's stressed beats; he knew what he was doing.

The Aim of the Game

To clarify thought and motivation, and pinpoint meaning within each line.

Skills
Articulation, Clarity, Connection

Personal Pronouns

A game to help actors locate the drama in the playwright's choice of vocabulary.

How to Play

This is a simple game in which the text is broken up into its constituent parts and dramatised, in order to find detail in the language.

Arrange the company into pairs or groups according to scenes (the smaller the groups, the better). They should begin by acting the scene in the normal manner, to get the sense of the journey and establish the basics of the scene.

Then ask them to play the scene again, but this time every time the actors hit a *personal pronoun* – for the purposes of the game that means any mention of a person or character, absent or present (I, you, he, she, they, we, Mr Spencer, Celia, the cow) – they must emphasise it and make a gesture to place the emphasis on that person, e.g. 'Gallop apace, *you* fiery-footed steeds.' They can point to them if they are in the scene, or offstage to wherever they might be if they are not, whilst letting the rest of the line go; not so it's inaudible, of course, but so the emphasis is on these specific words. Observe whether the characters use a similar number of personal pronouns, and look specifically at what they are and what that tells us about them. If a character mentions him or herself in almost every sentence (look at Bottom in *A Midsummer Night's Dream* as an example), it can tell us an awful lot about their personality.

Now, repeat the exercise but this time, instead of personal pronouns, the actors emphasise all the *adjectives* and *adverbs* (descriptive words). Any descriptive language counts, no matter where it is used in the sentence, e.g. 'Gallop *apace*, you *fiery-footed* steeds'. And, of course, mark each adjective with a gesture. This is where the game becomes dramatic. Look at the sort of language each character uses. Are they simple and to the point? Or flowery and gushing? How do they use description – and why? Are they trying to seduce, or impress, or rebuff? Perhaps they don't use any descriptive language at all. And if so, why not?

Finally, repeat the exercise but this time the players should emphasise all the *verbs* (doing words), marking each with a gesture: '*Gallop* apace, you fiery-footed steeds.' Encourage them to be bold and move with the gestures to capture the physical drama in the text. Each actor should observe how active their character is, and whether their language is exaggerated or simplistic.

A character's words are their tools. No one talks without an objective, so each actor should consider what their character intends to achieve by exploring how they speak. Over the three rounds of this exercise, the active, descriptive and personal language of each character will have come into focus. By the end, each actor should have a much better idea of how their character's mind works. They should continue to observe the frequency and style of these verbal characteristics throughout the text as they work on each scene. It will tell them a great deal about their character's personality.

The Aim of the Game

To investigate every character's language and through it find out more about them, their objectives and their relationships.

Skills
Analysis, Characterisation, Focus

Jazzercise

A game where the players scat-sing the text.

How to Play

Scat-singing is improvised jazz. When musicians improvise together they listen to each other in order to pick up on cues and work as an ensemble. And that is where actors may learn something from them.

There comes a point in most rehearsal processes where actors will know a scene so well that their manner of playing each line becomes ingrained. It moves into muscle memory and it can become difficult to deliver the line in any other way.

In order to prevent the over-learning of lines, which can lead to stale performances, try scat-singing it. Ask them to play the scene, singing the text instead of speaking it but, like jazz singers do, purposefully adding pauses, holding words, changing the rhythm in order to ensure other players can't predict their delivery. In doing so, they not only drop their regular rhythms, but the actors responding to them will have to rethink their delivery as the known patterns will be gone.

In some ways, this game is the opposite to the other text singing game in this book, *Shakespeare: The Musical!* (Game 10), in which the point is to find the recognisable and correct shape of a line. This exercise is all about going against what the text tells you and shaking it up. It is not only great fun, but it's hugely releasing and will, as a by-product, force the actors to listen to each other much more carefully.

The Aim of the Game

To shake up fixed patterns of speech and find new rhythms and cadences in the text, whilst also encouraging listening.

Skills
Improvisation, Rhythm, Spontaneity, Voice

Shadow Play

A game to free actors from the script by having a 'shadow' feed in the lines.

How to Play

It is always tricky for actors to find the freedom to move in early rehearsals, whilst they are still encumbered by having their scripts in hand. There is, however, an easy way to combat this. Put aside a day early in rehearsals to try this exercise.

Allocate a 'shadow' to each actor in the scene. Very simply, that shadow quietly feeds their actor his or her lines from the sidelines, standing at edge of the stage. This ensures the actors have the space to move around on stage. The shadows must give the actors their lines in digestible chunks, a line or phrase at a time. They must speak neutrally, with no emotional connection, reading without expression to give the actors in the scene the chance to interpret their own lines.

Encourage the actors to respond imaginatively to the prompts, playing around with their delivery. It is easy to get into patterns of line speaking as you learn the text. This exercise is an opportunity to shake it up, try a slightly different tone or intonation and really listen to the other actors in the scene. It is surprising how much freedom this exercise allows the actors, both in terms of finding their own voice and actively listening to their partners.

The Aim of the Game

To find truth and freshness in the text. By taking away the burden of holding their scripts, the actors can explore physical expression and spontaneous delivery unencumbered.

Skills
Characterisation, Listening, Spontaneity

28

The Obstacle Game

A host of exercises to take the pressure off the text in order to release the scene.

How to Play

Actors will often feel great pressure, when performing a scene in rehearsals, to get it 'right' – physically, vocally, emotionally – all at the same time. One way of combating this is to put an obstacle in the way – a physical task – in order to free the text. This not only takes the pressure off blocking the movement of the scene, but it mobilises the actor to discover a more spontaneous approach to the text. Play your scenes with the following obstacles. Most are designed for dialogue scenes, once the company have learnt their lines, but you can adapt all of them as you wish to suit ensemble or physical scenes.

1.

Ask the company to stand in a circle. Of the actors in the scene, ask the key protagonist to stand inside the circle, and the others in the scene to stay outside it (in a duologue you will therefore have one actor in and one outside the ring). The actor in the middle must try to break out to reach the other actor(s). The ensemble's aim is to stop them. If you don't have a large enough cast to make a circle, ask anyone else who is on hand to join in: stage management, you (!), etc.

2.

An exercise for two-person scenes. Ask the company to stand in a line, which goes from one wall to the opposite wall, dividing your playing space into two, and place one actor on each side of the wall. They players forming the wall should all touch, whether arm to arm or holding hands, in order to form a solid wall. The two actors now play the scene moving up and down and through the line, they can crawl between legs, play hide-and-seek along it, try and climb through it. Ask them to be as playful as possible and to use what's happening in the scene to inform whether they want to unite with, follow or escape from the other actor. You may choose to allow your wall to help or hinder the actors in their quest.

3.

Give the actors an activity. Baking a cake. Washing each other's hair. Playing a ball game. Make it something physical; if it's too small, like knitting, it's too easy to continue the scene in its usual manner. It can be most interesting when you give them an activity that needs two people, like Giant Jenga, for example, or playing a duet on the piano. The tensions and intimacies of the activity will inform, and sometimes interestingly clash with, the context of the scene.

4.

Ask the actors to stand at opposite ends of the room, as far from each other as possible. Ask the rest of the ensemble to find a space in the room. The actors should begin the scene, and as they do, try and meet in the middle of the room. The aim of the ensemble is to stop them.

5.

Play tag with the whole group and ask the two actors to continue their scene whilst everyone plays, including them.

The Aim of the Game

Each of these exercises takes the pressure off the actor to find a physical or emotional language to suit their scene. Instead, the physicality stems naturally from the tasks they are given, freeing them from the need for blocking and enabling them to make new discoveries about the shape, tone and emotional scale of the scene. Most of the exercises are designed to give the actors physical conflict to play against, which can help increase the heat in a scene. You can learn a great deal about the relationships in a scene by placing it in adversity.

Skills
Analysis, Characterisation, Focus

The Rubber Duck of Doom

Throw in some emotion-provoking props to spice up your scene.

How to Play

Early in rehearsals, actors may make decisions about how to play a particular moment emotionally. This game helps to prevent actors from locking down those choices too early. The aim is to play and have fun exploring rather than find a new interpretation, though you may discover something that you want to keep.

Are there any actual props in the scene? Is there tea to be poured, or a newspaper to be read? If so, use these props. If not, introduce some more. They could be sensible or silly: a rubber duck is my personal favourite. You should have four props all together. Allocate each prop an emotion, for example: anger, happiness, fear, sadness (hence the eponymous Rubber Duck of *Doom*).

Now, play the scene as usual – only with these props in play. Each time an actor is handed one of the props, they must express the emotion it carries with it, whether it fits in with their character or not. The props don't have to be used naturalistically; the actors should find excuses to pass them on to each other in order to make the scene as hard (and funny) as possible.

You can introduce the props one by one, or play with fewer if you want to look at a particular emotion in the scene. It is surprising, seeing as the roots of the game are comedic, that one can occasionally make important emotional discoveries when you realise, for example, that a heart-wrenching moment is more effectively played with lightness.

The Aim of the Game

To explore alternative emotional layers in a scene and experiment with feelings freely.

+ Selection of props
Skills
Characterisation, Improvisation, Spontaneity

PART THREE

THE WORLD OF THE PLAY

In which we look at the genre of the play and how to tackle it

'...Wow! That performance was... so subtle.'

How would you feel if that was your feedback in an audition? If you were up for a role in a modern drama, it might be exactly what you wanted to hear. But what if it was an audition for Restoration comedy? You can bet you won't be getting a recall. Why? Because the style of playing is completely different, and whilst every form of theatre demands emotional connection, depth of understanding and truthfulness, there's no denying that different genres require specific acting styles.

For me, a great actor is someone who captures the *style* of the text brilliantly. The best actors create their performance according to the stylistic demands of the script, and play a devastating Lady Macbeth, a hilarious Mrs Malaprop and an electrifying Medea in completely different ways. It's essential to understand that the form of Naturalism that Stanislavski favoured would look underpowered and flat in a heightened Greek tragedy. So, having investigated the text in Part Two, the next step is to consider the period and style of writing in order to understand the genre and how to play it.

Part Three is divided into seven genre-specific sections. The genres are by no means exclusive; there are a plethora of alternative ways of dividing theatre history, but between them these seven cover all the essential bases, and if you are playing a style that doesn't fall exactly into one of the categories, it most likely borrows from a combination of them. For example, if you are rehearsing a pantomime you can draw on *Physical Theatre and Commedia dell'Arte*, *Early Modern Comedy* or *Restoration and Georgian Comedy*, whichever you find more useful. Similarly, if you're rehearsing a modern play with tragic or epic elements, like Simon Stephen's *Motortown*, George Büchner's *Woyzeck* or Anne Washburn's *Mr Burns*, you might draw on *Greek Tragedy* and *Modern Drama and Naturalism*.

Consider the big ideas in the play too, as they might lead you to explore other chapters. Laura Wade's contemporary play *Posh* focuses on the behaviour of a pack of rich young men. By using the chorus exercises in the *Greek Tragedy* section, you could help the actors focus on ensemble playing to create the sense of unison. Modern plays are often inspired by earlier forms too, the study of which can hugely improve your understanding of the play. Mike Bartlett's *King Charles III* is similar to a Shakespearean history play in its form and approach to its subject, Richard Bean's *One Man, Two Guvnors* is inspired by Carlo Goldoni's *A Servant of Two Masters* and absolutely requires a knowledge of *Commedia* in its rehearsal, and my own play *Nell Gwynn* is about Restoration theatre and requires a understanding of heightened comedy in its performance.

In *Greek Tragedy*, we look at the building blocks of the genre, specifically the use of the chorus, mask and tableaux, alongside investigating the themes of hierarchy and power.

In *Shakespeare and His Contemporaries*, we focus on the use of verse and language, explore how to find life in the text and speak it effectively. We look at iambic pentameter and blank verse in detail, in addition to Shakespeare's comedy, then finish by looking at how to paraphrase in order to fully understand meaning in a complex text (and there's an example of an exercise that could be applied to any well-written play).

In *Restoration and Georgian Comedy*, we look at the specific relationship with the audience built in to these early comedies, how to engage with the audience and how to manage asides. We also look at the themes that define the genre: marriage, love and scandalous gossip.

In *Physical Theatre and Commedia dell' Arte*, clowning and comic characterisation are explored, as well as the dance-like quality of *Commedia*. Some exercises encourage actors to use their bodies as instruments, whilst others focus on comic improvisation and quick-thinking.

The *Early Modern Comedy* section gives actors the tools to play the verbal wit and dexterity of the period. The plays of Oscar Wilde and Noël Coward, for example, are full of razor-sharp sparring matches. Some games in this section encourage the precision and speed of repartee, whilst other investigate the conventions of the genre: the pack behaviour, stock characters and social themes.

The section on *Modern Drama and Naturalism* aims to give actors a toolkit to tackle emotional realism, which we associate with the titans of late nineteenth- and early twentieth-century drama, like Chekhov, Ibsen and Shaw, but which are equally as important in exploring the work of contemporary writers who aim for realism, like Mike Leigh. The exercises focus on spontaneity, truthfulness, backstory and character analysis.

Finally, the chapter on *New Plays* aims to help actors and directors who are working with a writer on the first production of a previously unperformed play. The games focus on interrogating the story for the entire creative team, the actors and, where appropriate, the writer, in order to work towards a final performance script. The exercises focus on character journey and play structure (exercises which, while essential in workshopping a new play, are also great in any rehearsal process to help form an overview of the action). They ask the actors to consider what happens between the written scenes and to explore their characters and the worlds they exist in.

Whilst the aim of dividing the chapter into genre-based sections is to ensure you have tools to tackle the specific play you're working on, I would wholeheartedly encourage you to explore other categories too. Games in *Modern Drama and Naturalism* look at creating character detail, for example; useful skills for any actor. Similarly, there are three sections that focus on comedy, and whilst you will most likely want to focus on the games designed for your genre, you will find each offers exercises on physical and verbal dexterity. Every role benefits from being played with truth and heart, so the exercises on Shakespeare, modern drama and new plays can all be used to encourage connection.

To help you choose which games to play, you'll find a *Skills Index* at the back of the book, which lists games according to the skills they enhance.

Play around with the games; adapt them and make them your own. They are a box of toys to be shaken up, broken, stuck back together and tossed over the floor. Make a glorious mess.

Greek Tragedy

Ancient Greek theatre is the great-great-grandparent of modern theatre. The branches of many of our contemporary traditions stem from its roots. It famously gave us the genres of comedy and tragedy, use of masks and choral speaking, but it also contributed a whole host of less commonly attributed theatrical staples, like the trapdoor and flying. The fifth century BCE was a pretty exciting time in terms of theatremaking, and it all began when actors gathered to present stories in honour of their god Dionysus, patron of wine, fertility and theatre. An excellent triumvirate.

In Greek theatre, tragedy most specifically, we find elements of theatrical convention we take for granted as the building blocks of drama, but which, before that period, may not have existed in the same manner. The Ancient Greeks were the first to institutionalise theatre, organising public performances at a set time of day which required the audience to buy a ticket. They invented the concept of a theatrical auditorium and were the first to make acting a profession. They celebrated their playwrights and defined tragedy and comedy as the two principal genres of story. It is a testament to their skill as dramatists that their plays stand up today.

Every year, at the Theatre of Dionysus in Ancient Athens, three playwrights were pitted against each other to write three tragedies and a satyr (a category which would evolve into 'comedy'). Early plays only had one actor, the first recorded being Thespis (hence 'thespian'), though over time the number of actors in a play increased to three. Realising how popular the form was, the Greeks soon decided to export their theatre festival across the globe, and touring theatre was born.

Though many of the original plays were lost over time (and when the Great Library of Alexandria was burnt, one of the travesties of early history), it is remarkable how many plays have survived. Sophocles, Aeschylus, Aristophanes and Euripides all wrote plays that are still performed and studied today. *Oedipus Rex*, *Medea*, *Antigone*, *Iphigenia*, *The Oresteia* and *Women of Troy* still form a regular part of the contemporary repertoire. And why? Because they are dramatic plots with boldly written characters, epic journeys and tragic events to play. For an actor, the chance to play a Greek hero is a real treat.

In terms of character, Greek drama is peopled with tragic characters who have great obstacles to overcome. Often featuring gods, kings and queens, young royals and warriors, the stories tend to focus on dramatic themes like treachery and justice, and often feature murder, war and familial betrayal. Actors approaching these roles will need to be equipped to play the dramatic scenes with both the required scale of deeply felt emotion, and to find truth and heart in the drama. These are great challenges for any actor, and explain why so many performers are keen to take on these titanic roles.

The following exercises introduce the key concepts of the Greek traditions. The genre is vast so I make no pretentions to suggest that the games provide a complete education on the subject, but as starting points, they provide a way to dip in your theatrical toe and avoid your Achilles heel.

The two practices that most strongly characterise Greek tragedy are use of the chorus and mask work. The chorus are a group of characters who often speak in unison (choral speaking) and comment on the action. Representing the community, they provide a sense of how the action of the play impacts on the wider world. Often townsfolk, but sometimes gods or animals, the chorus provide a commentary, which presents context and opinions, helping the audience understand what has happened before the action begins, between scenes and, sometimes, an epilogue to reveal the consequences of the drama. They may also provide a comic foil or add in other ways, using song, for example, to enhance the production. As an element of performance, a chorus can be a great asset. They provide an engaged theatrical spectacle, which directors and actors enjoy experimenting with, providing atmosphere, visual drama and sometimes music in order to accentuate the narrative.

Use of masks, which began with the Greeks, has also become a celebrated theatrical tradition. Playing in huge auditoria, Greek actors wore masks in order to help the audience identify which character they were playing, so that they could play a number of different roles and be identified from a distance. With exaggerated expressions, the mask also suggested the character's personality; often comic masks were grotesque in order to provide humour. They were carefully designed to act like small megaphones in order to help transmit the words to the back rows. However, they were more than merely practical tools. Masks allow actors to transform physically, since, with their faces covered, the actors must use their bodies to portray a character vividly. They also provide visual spectacle when used as a group. A chorus which moves and speaks with synchronicity, with identical faces, can be a thrilling image.

In addition to chorus and mask work, Greek theatre is also celebrated for its use of the *ekkyklema* (a portable stage for delivering tableaux) to deliver a dramatic punch. In *The Ekkyklema* exercise, we look at how such tableaux can be used to express moments of great drama through a frozen image. The Greeks understood the much-loved maxim that less is more when you are asking the audience to imagine horror.

In *Morus Chorus*, we introduce aspects of choral work. This is taken a step further in my favourite game title in the book, *Bryan Adams in a Toga*, in which you apply the elements you've learnt in choral work to explore the modern equivalent of a tragic monologue. In *Mask Play*, you'll find a host of beginner exercises to familiarise yourselves with masks, and some improvisations to combine this with ensemble work. Finally, *King of the Parthenon* explores the theme of hierarchy that runs through all the plays of the period.

There are other aspects of Greek staging I haven't covered here. The Greeks were tireless inventors. They were fond of trapdoors and enjoyed surprising the audience by bringing actors up from the depths. They were also the first of many daredevil theatremakers to use flying; they invented a crane called a *mechane* to lift the actor (often playing a god) clean off the stage. Both of these elements reflect the Greek's obsession with mortals versus gods, a recurring theme in all of their plays. I haven't written an exercise using cranes or trapdoors for fear of being sued... but if you want to make up your own, be my guest. Just don't blame me.

The Ekkyklema

How to use tableaux to explore potent images.

How to Play

In Greek drama, unlike in most modern drama, playwrights often used characters or choruses to report the dramatic action, rather than show it unfolding on stage, thereby encouraging the audiences to imagine the (often tragic) scenarios. When reporting action which took place in interior spaces, they sometimes used a piece of equipment called an *ekkyklema*: a wooden platform they wheeled out of the skene (the hut behind the playing area) onto the stage. On it the actors would stand in a frozen pictures, or tableaux, to give the audience an image of the action of that key moment. Some scholars think it may have revolved, to allow the audience to fully appreciate the image from every angle, before it wheeled back offstage.

Consider the dramatic advantages of showing drama in a still image rather than a full scene. Of course, for some of the horrendous acts in Greek tragedy – the gouging-out of eyes, or the killing of children – there may be the practical advantage of avoiding the difficulty of staging them. But more importantly, a tableau can provide a clear still image, the visible part of the iceberg, which allows the audience to do most of the imagining. Just like a good novel, the skill is in asking the audience to picture something worse than could be shown on stage. The imagination is a remarkably powerful tool.

Try tableaux for yourself:

As a warm-up, split the group into teams, give them an image to make and countdown from ten. They must be frozen in position by zero. You can give them easy challenges to start them off – a flowerpot, a fruit bowl. Or tableaux which require some gymnastics – a bridge, a see-saw. But once they've done a few simple objects to limber up, move on to the themes of the play. Try images of justice, revenge, grief, war, love. Consider whether the results work better when they are images from the story, peopled with characters and events, or when they are more abstract – a symbolic representation of a theme.

Then, pick the key dramatic moments of the text you are working on. Mark out an ekkyklema in chalk on the floor, and give your actors time to create stirring tableaux of each key moment. Try inserting these into your text and see what the effect is. As a further exercise it can also be interesting to use tableaux between scenes to reveal the offstage action, or to try telling your whole play through a series of silent images.

The Aim of the Game

To begin using the Greek conventions whilst exploring themes and relationships on stage. For this reason, you can use this exercise to explore any play, not only the Greeks, because it encourages the actors to boil down a story to its key dramatic moments, and to explore the related themes through physical expression.

Skills
Ensemble Work, Imagination, Pace

Morus Chorus

A game which uses the Greek notion of a chorus to encourage the company to work as an ensemble.

How to Play

The most recognisable feature of a Greek tragedy is the chorus. When performed well, a chorus can be a fantastic theatrical coup at the centre of a production. Try this simple exercise as a way to develop the ensemble relationship within your chorus.

Ask the players to form a diamond shape, facing the front. One person at the apex, two people in the line behind, then (for example if you are using nine players), three in the centre line, two behind them and one at the back. If you have extra players you can adjust the number of players in the middle lines to include everyone.

Begin with the group facing the front. The chorus leader is the person at the apex of the diamond, closest to the audience. That player should begin moving slowly, in motions flowing enough to be copied smoothly. The rest of the group must try and copy exactly, moving simultaneously so that the audience would not be able to detect who was leading. The leader should begin moving on the spot, making small movements, one limb at a time, e.g. raising an arm, flexing a foot, rolling the head. Then they can start exploring the space, moving forwards and backwards, until they are all moving around as a flowing ensemble mass.

Now, you should build in changes of direction. If your chorus turns ninety degrees to face stage left, they will find they have a new leader – the person on the far left of the middle row in the original diamond. That player now inherits the leadership and must seamlessly take over the movement in a way that is invisible to the audience. Each time the leader faces either ninety degrees to the left or right, or even the back wall, the leadership of the chorus will change.

This game has some elements in common with *The Boogie Pyramid* (Game 22), but their aims are quite different, so if you are playing both, do ensure the focus here is on synchronised movement, encouraging the ensemble to move as one. *The Boogie Pyramid*, in contrast, is about having fun with scale and physicality.

Variation

If you're really ambitious, you can add sound. If you are working with a Greek text, the actors could speak their choral text as the exercise is played. Begin each new line on each new movement. This will encourage the actors to work wholly as a unit, both vocally and physically. If you don't have choral text, either use a song everyone knows, or use the alphabet – speak each new letter at the beginning of every new movement, or every time the group faces a new direction, in order to synchronise as one.

The Aim of the Game

To work as an ensemble to become a seamlessly coordinated chorus, with no indication as to who is leading, as if they are one body.

Skills
Ensemble Work, Focus, Physicality

Bryan Adams in a Toga

A game to explore the voice of the chorus using a nineties classic.

How to Play

The term 'choral work ' strikes fear into the heart of many actors; there's something about it that sounds terribly serious and feels like it should be approached with a straight back, a portentous voice and a great deal of caution. In reality, this isn't the case at all. The presence of a chorus on stage can be thrilling, not only for their contribution to the drama, but because of the fun you can have experimenting with a shared voice. In terms of choral speaking, it's worth spending some time exploring the potential for sound effects and characterisation in the way your chorus delivers their lines. But leave behind the intimidating tragic texts for a moment, and begin with the exact opposite – lyrics from a cheesy nineties classic. All hail Bryan Adams.

Give the company copies of the lyrics from '(Everything I Do) I Do It for You'. If you don't know them already then you can easily find them online. Believe it or not, there is a reason for choosing this specific song. It has all the elements of a Greek tragedy: it is epic, it uses universals, life and death are ever-present and its singer will sacrifice everything for the cause of love. Who knew Bryan Adams and Oedipus had so much in common (though thankfully Adams isn't singing about his mother)?

Split the group into two teams. Ask them to create a choral version of the song, adhering to the following rules:

- Speak, don't sing, the lyrics.
- There must be a minimum of two people speaking at once.
- You must use repetition as an echo, whether whole lines or single words.
- You must use pause or silence for effect.
- You must speak part of the song as a whole ensemble.

- You must have a call and response, where part of the song is split into conversation.

- You must vary the dynamics. Think of modulation: volume, pitch, pace, tone.

- You must select characters to play. Don't let it be general: who are you and why are you saying these words?

Give the two teams fifteen minutes to create these epic works and then share them. Consider what was effective and what didn't work. Then repeat the exercise with your Greek text. You can bet choral speaking is less intimidating now.

Variation

There are plenty of other songs that work well for this game too, so choose your own. Power ballads are the best. Pick one with dramatic statements, universal imagery and big ideas. Think Tina Turner or Gloria Gaynor rather than Jack Johnson or Kate Nash. Here's a few to inspire you.

- 'I Will Survive' by Gloria Gaynor.

- 'Don't Stop Believin'' by Journey.

- 'Always' by Bon Jovi.

- 'I'd Do Anything for Love (But I Won't Do That)' by Meat Loaf.

- 'Tragedy' by the Bee Gees.

- 'Think' by Aretha Franklin.

The Aim of the Game

To explore the voice and character of the chorus in a light-hearted but insightful way.

Skills
Characterisation, Ensemble Work, Rhythm, Voice

Mask Play

A game that uses masks to help unlock character and physicality.

How to Play

In addition to being great fun in its own right, mask work can benefit an actor as it tests so many performance skills. Specifically, it demands clarity in the transmission of emotions. As we cannot see a masked actor's eyes, he or she must use their body to communicate what they are feeling.

For the following exercises you can use neutral masks (with no expression) or character masks. If you are looking for the latter, I'd recommend Trestle Theatre Company's masks, which you can order online. This series of exercises covers the basic elements of mask work. None require speech so encourage the actors to focus purely on physical expression as you give them the following instructions:

1. Get to know your mask. Look at it, consider its character. Pull your face into the same expression as the mask and consider how it affects your posture.

2. Allow the mask's expression to flow through your entire body. Does it raise or lower your shoulders? Does it swell your chest or make you hunch? Does it push your hips forwards confidently or pull you back in retreat? What does it do to your knees? Do they point forward, ready to set off, or move outwards in confusion?

3. Move around the space with the mask on. Where is your weight? Is it forward and active or pulling towards your ankles? Are you boldly 'on the front foot' or nervously trying to disappear? As you move, focus on each different part of your body and play around in order to find a body that fits the face, and a movement that fits the body.

4. Masks lose their character once we see the sides of them as the illusion is broken. Try to move around the space keeping the majority

of your face to the front. Avoid touching them too, as the contrast between a real hand and an unreal mask is distracting.

5. Move across the space one by one. When you reach the middle, you must notice something that changes your emotion. Your body should reveal the change. Allow us to see, from your physical transformation, the specific reaction to your discovery. Have you seen someone you love? Have you spied some food, or a bag of money? Have you remembered something you should have done, realising you're going to be in deep trouble? Have you seen a ghost? The trick is to communicate the changing emotion through your body alone, as you cannot change your facial expression.

6. Improvise a scene in pairs. Choose which of you has the higher status (if you're using expressive masks, then one will probably have a naturally higher status). Play out a wordless scene in which the power balance must reverse. For example, if your set-up is an angry customer returning some ill-fitting shoes to a nervous shop assistant, something must happen within the scene to conclude it with the nervous character 'winning'. Does she seduce him? Does she humiliate him by smelling the shoes? It sounds simple, but working without words can be quite a challenge.

7. Improvise a scene with half the cast, so that the other half can watch and thus learn how mask work can be played most effectively. Try one of the following scenarios and encourage the actors to commit fully to their characters:

- The hospital waiting room in A and E.
- A speed-dating night.
- An airport lounge.
- A station platform at midnight on a Friday.
- A bread queue in a war zone.

If you are working with neutral masks then ask the actors to make a bold emotional choice to give themselves a feeling to start with: elation, frustration, anxiety. If you are working with character masks then try to use a range of masks so that multiple dynamics are brought into play.

These are all simple exercises, but each encourages the players to be specific and bold in their choices. It's vital in mask work that, before you begin incorporating dialogue, you have learnt to communicate physically. Bear in mind that Greek amphitheatres seated fifteen thousand people, so the physical gestures of those early actors would have had to communicate over a great distance. Use that as inspiration to aim for clarity of movement and message.

Variation

Once you feel the actors have gained confidence then you might like to add dialogue, particularly if you are using half-masks (some full masks are designed specifically for mime and you'll find you can't speak with them on!). Emotionally wrought situations are often best. Try giving each pair the first line for an improvisation, which leads them into a dramatic scenario. Make sure the line gives them a strong enough starting point. For example:

- 'I've waited my whole life to tell you this…'
- 'Don't do it… don't jump!'
- 'Whatever you do, don't turn around.'
- 'I saw what you did – don't even try and deny it.'

The Aim of the Game

To introduce mask work and heighten an awareness of physicality as a tool for communication and characterisation.

+ Set of masks
Skills
Characterisation, Communication, Physicality

King of the Parthenon

Consider your character's place in the world.

How to Play

The plot of many classical plays relates to the hierarchy of the characters. Many Greek plays feature a challenge to leadership, whether it's a child defying their elders (*Antigone*), the rise of a flawed hero against fate (*Oedipus*), or the women in society struggling at the hands of their successors (*Women of Troy*). Drama is about conflict, and conflict is almost always about power, or lack of it.

It's essential to work out the hierarchy of the characters in your play at the beginning of your rehearsal process. Even if each character's status isn't projected outwardly, the entire company must know how everyone relates to everyone else. Laurence Olivier famously quipped that in order to play a king, he didn't need to do anything; he just needed everyone else to treat him as the king.

Working out the hierarchy may well require research. In Ancient Greece, for example, the gods dominated the highest tiers of the social hierarchy, followed by mortals; within that men dominated women, and fortune triumphed over poverty – but gender was such a disadvantage that a rich female had fewer rights than a poor man, despite her fortune. Women weren't even allowed to go to the theatre in Ancient Athens, let alone take part in it.

Working out a hierarchy is always complex because it can be considered from so many perspectives: social, financial, birth, etc. In order to explore it practically, ask the cast to order themselves (as their characters) in a line according to some of the following hierarchical structures, depending on the focus of the play you're working on:

- How much you're worth financially.
- What your social standing is.
- How popular you are.
- How eligible you are as a potential partner.
- How powerful you are.
- How moral you are.

- How intelligent you are.
- How hardworking you are.
- How religious you are.
- How trusted you are.

Be prepared for a great deal of debate, and perhaps a feud or two! It can be interesting, once you have done this, to number the actors with a status from I to I0 and ask them to play that very strongly within a scene. See how it refocuses the scene on power play and group dynamics. The actors should say their lines as they are written, but observe the way in which they might change the way they play them, and sometimes even the implication of a line. It can add a level of depth previously unexplored.

The Aim of the Game

To encourage a deeper understanding of character, both in terms of the individual and the dynamics of the group, and to explore the historical context of the play.

Skills
Analysis, Characterisation, Ensemble Work

Shakespeare and
His Contemporaries

    '…Do you know how to speak verse?'

  '…Is that a masculine or a feminine ending?'

      '…Use the iambic pentameter.'

The notion that there's one way to perform Shakespearean text 'properly' can be terribly intimidating to the inexperienced actor. Terms like 'blank verse' and 'metre' are bandied about without explanation, leaving some actors feeling certain that there's some secret method which must be understood in order to do it right. It's true. There is. But there's nothing scary about it; in fact, the rules are remarkably simple.

The games in this section are intended to demystify the plays of Shakespeare, his contemporaries – Christopher Marlowe, Ben Jonson and John Webster, amongst many others – and those who followed. We look specifically about the notion of verse, considering what 'iambic pentameter' is (his most common form), how to speak it and why it is used.

The games here focus primarily on form rather than character because to try and describe Shakespeare's characters as fitting into any one bracket would be entirely reductive. His plays are peopled with everyone from the heroes of Henry IV, the tragic figures like Macbeth and Hamlet, to comic wits like Benedick and Beatrice, alongside philosophers like Jaques in *As You Like It*, the clever Fools in *King Lear* and *Twelfth Night*, and the young lovers of *Romeo and Juliet* and *Love's Labour's Lost*. The one trait they all have in common is that they are three-dimensional, carefully written parts that are a joy to delve into. Actors have often returned to the same play, even to the same part, more than once in their career, so much is there to explore in any single role. Alongside Shakespeare, his contemporaries wrote similarly complex roles. From Webster's Duchess of Malfi, who finds herself entwined in a web of love, patriarchy and deceit, to the delightful comic tricksters in Jonson's *The Alchemist*, who set out on a fraudulent mission to con every gullible Londoner they meet, the characters in this genre all present exciting challenges, requiring verbal dexterity in the playing of verse, strong character choices and a connection to emotional truth.

We begin the chapter with *Improvised Pentameter*, which breaks down the notion of 'verse' and asks actors to use it in their own way before they begin to approach the text.

Bard Ball applies these verse skills to the speaking of Shakespeare's language. We look at regular blank verse and the common alternatives, to equip actors with the basic tools to recognise verse types and know how to speak them. We also touch on line length – masculine and feminine endings – to investigate how these specific choices reflect a character's emotional state.

Knotty-pated Fools is a game which celebrates Shakespeare's imaginative use of insults, and gives actors the chance to fling their own verbal mud around. *Stepping Stones* focuses on the structure of a speech, with an emphasis on using punctuation. Finally, *In Your Own Words* is a paraphrasing game that encourages actors to translate their text into modern English, in order to be sure they understand every word.

These games are designed to give you a flavour of the joy of working on Shakespearean text, or indeed any text in verse. There is no shortage of brilliant books on the subject. I always refer back to the feted works of Cicely Berry, Patsy Rodenburg and Barbara Houseman, to name but a few. I would also recommend *Speaking the Speech*, a fabulous book by Shakespeare's Globe's Master of Words, Giles Block. So use these exercises as a starting point, before exploring the work in depth.

Improvised Pentameter

An easy way to feel Shakespeare's rhythms by improvising them yourselves.

How to Play

Everyone stands in a circle. First, establish what iambic pentameter is and how it works. It is the rhythm most commonly used by Shakespeare, and it sounds like a heartbeat. An iamb is a pair of beats, a weak beat followed by a strong beat, giving us the 'de-DUM' of a heartbeat. Five iambs (de-DUMs) in a row gives us 'pentameter,' so iambic pentameter is a ten-beat line, consisting of five de-DUMs. Begin by tapping out the iambic pentameter on your chest – like so:

De-DUM, de-DUM, de-DUM, de-DUM, de-DUM.

Repeat this until the group is comfortable with this rhythm. Now see if you can throw in some Shakespeare lines that fit this pattern. If you have experienced actors, go round the circle, asking everyone to throw in a line. If not, you can give some examples yourself and ask the group to repeat them.

'The COURSE of TRUE love NEVer DID run SMOOTH.'

'If MUSic BE the FOOD of LOVE, play ON!'

'The LADy DOTH proTEST too MUCH, meTHINKS.'

Try and give the sentences a sense of real speech as much as possible whilst still using the rhythm.

Now, break the circle up and ask the group to sustain the rhythm as they walk around the room, stepping on every strong beat. As they go, ask them to improvise lines of their own.

'PerHAPS you'd LIKE a CUP of TEA with ME?'

'I WONder, COULD I ASK you FOR a DRINK?'

'The CAfé SHUTS at THREE, so NOW we're CLOSED.'

'I LIKE your DOG. What KIND of DOG is HE?'

What is fascinating is that you'll probably find the keywords in a sentence tend to be the stressed words, without even trying:

'I LIKE your DOG. What KIND of DOG is HE?'

All the important words – *like, dog, kind, he* – are naturally stressed. The others are less significant – *I, your, what, of, is*. The English language naturally falls into the cadences of iambic pentameter so you'll probably find it easier to improvise than you'd expect.

Now, ask the group to get into pairs and choose a scenario: painting a wall, cooking a risotto, ordering dinner at a restaurant, meeting a long-lost relative, anything they want. Then they should improvise the scene in iambic pentameter.

Once everyone has done so, you might like to mix it up by breaking the rules, as Shakespeare does. Whilst most of his verse is strictly iambic pentameter (i.e. ten syllables in the line), sometimes you will find a line has an extra syllable, or one fewer than normal, either way ending on an unstressed syllable. He hasn't slipped up; it is deliberate and it's known as a feminine ending because it is weak (how rude!). These feminine endings are used to give a particular effect. For example, an extra syllable can make a thought hang over into the next line as though the speaker can't quite cope with the whole idea, thus leaving it unresolved.

'To BE or NOT to BE that IS the QUES...*tion*.'

The extra syllable hangs on incomplete, like a nagging doubt, which is exactly how Hamlet is feeling. It makes the word 'question' stand out and linger. Imagine if, instead, Shakespeare had stuck to iambic pentameter and written the following:

'To BE or NOT to BE that IS the CRUX.'

Hamlet doesn't sounds nearly so confused! This well-formed thought sounds much more orderly and complete. In fact, that famous speech is peppered with feminine endings:

'Whether 'tis nobler in the mind to suf-*fer*
The slings and arrows of outrageous for-*tune*
Or to take arms against a sea of trou-*bles*
And by opposing, end them...'

'End them'... where's the rest of the line? He goes on, after a beat, 'To die, to sleep', but 'end them' is very much the end of the thought and is deliberately placed halfway through the line to make it stick out and feel uncomfortable. Thus Hamlet, envisioning the idea of death, is literally stopped by the verse, before he can go on.

Shakespeare also plays other tricks with half-lines. Sometimes he allows another character to pick up the second half of a line, thus stealing the end of someone's line. This is usually for one of two reasons. Either the interrupter won't let the other character finish through anger or tension – because they want to propel the other character to act. Lady Macbeth, for example, grabs the end of Macbeth's lines in retaliation:

MACBETH:

> Prithee, peace:
> I dare do all that may become a man;
> Who dares do more is none.

LADY MACBETH:

>   What beast was't, then,
> That made you break this enterprise to me?

This has the effect of showing her power to literally take his voice, mid-thought, and bend him to her will.

The other common reason for line sharing is love. When one character feels so passionate about the other, they may not be able to resist joining in with them, and even sharing their thoughts. In *Twelfth Night*, Orsino regularly finishes Viola's lines to reveal his enthusiasm for both her and her quest.

VIOLA:

> Sir, shall I to this lady?

ORSINO:

>   Aye, that's the theme.

Arrange the group back into their pairs to try another improvisation, but this time each actor should throw in half-lines for their partner to finish, and experiment with adding feminine endings to help articulate part-thoughts.

Finally, after this series of exercises, go back to the Shakespearean text, mark the pentameter on the text (put-tíng a márk abóve the stréss each tíme) and take note of any points at which Shakespeare chooses to employ a different shape, either feminine endings, half-lines or prose. Prose, or regular non-rhymed speech (normal conversation), is most often used to show a character's low or comic status, like the Mechanicals in *A Midsummer Night's Dream* or the porter in *Macbeth*. It sets those characters aside from the loftier aristocrats, intellects or lovers of the rest of the play. However, Shakespeare also uses it at points to reveal a moment of straightforward, undecorated language when a character has lost the power of poetry. For example, Hamlet's speech in Act Two, Scene Two:

> 'I have of late – but wherefore I know not – lost all my mirth, forgone all custom of exercise; and indeed it goes so heavily with my disposition that this goodly frame, the earth, seems to me a sterile promontory.'

The quality of everyday speech with which Hamlet speaks here reflects the fact he has dropped any façade or poetic artifice and instead expresses himself, simply and purely from the heart.

The Aim of the Game

To become aware of Shakespeare's specific use of rhythm and verse forms, and learn how to apply this to the speaking of text.

Skills
Improvisation, Rhythm, Verse-speaking

Bard Ball

Think basketball, but using verse.

How to Play

Ask the group to get into pairs with someone with whom they have dialogue in a scene. If the scene has more than two people in it, then ask the group to stand in a circle.

Very simply, each actor bounces the ball on the ground on each strong beat of the iambic pentameter.

'But SOFT what LIGHT through YONder WINdow BREAKS?'

They bounce the ball between themselves so that, when one person's line is finished, their partner can easily catch (or snatch, depending on the tone of the scene) the ball as it comes back up, in order to begin their line.

The idea is to be aware of the pattern of interaction written into the verse. If it has neat, full lines of iambic pentameter with masculine endings, the actor can finish the line and politely passes the ball on, simply and rhythmically. However, if the pair are in a verbal sparring match, one might swipe the ball from the other player at the end of their line, in order to give a spikey retort.

The game becomes most interesting when speaking in half-lines, where the ball is passed part-way through a line of iambic pentameter. The following snippet shows how Shakespeare sometimes divides lines into single syllables to build a sense of tension and desperation:

LADY MACBETH:
   I heard the owl scream and the crickets cry.
   Did you not speak?

MACBETH:
                     When?

LADY MACBETH:
                     Now?

MACBETH:
                          As I descended.

LADY MACBETH:
                               Ay.

MACBETH:
> Hark! Who lies i' the second chamber?

LADY MACBETH:
> Donalbain.

Here, the characters snatch the ball on almost every beat. Look at what that does to the physical state of tension, and how that dictates their relationship. When players have completed their scene, ask them to assess the power balance between them. Did one person do all the snatching? Did the power shift as the scene progressed? Or was it an evenly balanced love scene where the pair were delighted to hear what the other had to say?

If you have time, ask a couple of pairs to demonstrate – ideally pairs with contrasting verse shapes. The way the 'match' ensues is a clear demonstration of Shakespeare's variety of verse techniques and can make this otherwise intimidating form easier to understand.

The Aim of the Game

To increase awareness of the verse shape in the text, and to inform an understanding of the relationship between characters according to the rhythmic interplay of the lines.

+ Tennis balls
Skills
Ensemble Work, Rhythm, Verse-speaking

Knotty-pated Fools

A Shakespearean insult-slinging game.

How to Play

Before you begin, and ideally before this rehearsal session, ask the group to scour Shakespeare for their favourite insults and bring a list with them. Alternatively, you might provide examples yourself at the beginning of the session. Share them and talk about why they are effective. *Henry IV, Part I* is one of the best sources, as Falstaff is forever at the centre of rough exchanges:

'Thou clay-brained guts, thou knotty-pated fool, thou whoreson obscene greasy tallow-catch!'

'That trunk of humours, that bolting-hutch of beastliness, that swollen parcel of dropsies, that huge bombard of sack, that stuffed cloak-bag of guts, that roasted Manningtree ox with pudding in his belly, that reverend vice, that grey Iniquity, that father ruffian, that vanity in years?'

'You starvelling, you eel-skin, you dried neat's-tongue, you bull's-pizzle, you stock-fish – O for breath to utter what is like thee! You tailor's-yard, you sheath, you bow-case, you vile standing tuck!'

'Peace, ye fat guts!'

Ask the group to split into two and form lines facing each other. They are now enemies in a word battle.

Starting at one end of the line, the first player steps forward and gives a one-syllable insult to the person opposite them. They don't have to be Shakespearean, but they should be similarly inventive and vitriol-filled, for example:

'You boar!'

'You sheath!'

'You wart!'

The player opposite then sends a one-syllable insult back to the first player's immediate neighbour, thus moving play up the line.

Go the whole way up the line with single-syllable insults, then return back the other way with two syllables:

'You pizzle!'

'You muck weed!'

'You sheep fart!'

'You blockhead!'

Then repeat with two-word insults, an adjective then a noun:

'You muddled flump!'

'You rancid hole!'

'You pustulant toad!'

Then repeat with three-word insults, two adjectives and a noun:

'You petty piddle thief!'

'You rotten-egged puff!'

'You worm-infested gout!'

Then repeat with the word 'of' in the middle, as in:

'You swollen parcel of dropsies!'

'You huge bombard of sack!'

Finally, take the restrictions away and give each player the chance to throw one long insult across the room, where they riff on one breath, being as vile and as rude as they possibly can.

Of course, one would hope that players, be they professional actors or students, will be mature enough to treat this exercise strictly as a game. However, if necessary do ask them to make sure they're never personal with their insults – the further away from real life, the better!

The Aim of the Game

To appreciate Shakespeare's inventiveness and language, to gain a sense of the importance of rhythm in delivery and to let imaginations run wild.

Skills

Articulation, Imagination, Improvisation, Vocabulary

Stepping Stones

How to beat out the shape of the lines, step by step.

How to Play

This essential exercise has probably been taught in every drama school since Cicely Berry began her seminal teaching on the actor's relationship with the text.

Ask everyone to find a space in the room. The actors must now consider the shape of their lines and the pattern of their thoughts, by following your instructions, as follows:

Speak your line, walking in a straight line until you reach a punctuation mark.

If it is a full stop, then stop walking. Pause. Take a beat, then head off again at the start of your next sentence in a different direction. Mark the difference in the thought by the degree to which you change direction. If you're having a reversal of opinion, turn around and head off in the direction you came. If you're moving forward with the argument, continue in broadly the same direction.

If you reach a mid-line punctuation mark, like a comma, a semi-colon or an ellipsis, then change direction at that point. But don't stop, you must continue the flow of the line. Instead, just give yourself a slight hiatus as you switch direction. As above, choose the degree to which you change direction according to how great a change of idea you are having. If you are listing things in the same vein, or backing up a thought, then the change will be slight as the thoughts follow on and build on a theme.

Try to walk in a manner which reflects the punctuation. If the sentences short and definite with curt endings, move with purpose, boldly, quickly and in straight lines. If your thoughts are meandering, then allow this to influence how you walk.

The Aim of the Game

To use the punctuation to inform the thought processes and to reveal the shape of the text.

Skills
Analysis, Focus, Rhythm

In Your Own Words

A simple game to clarify meaning.

How to Play

One of my very first tasks when I'm rehearsing a classical play is to paraphrase the text into modern English, line by line, with the entire cast. It's so easy to miss this stage, but it's often not until you ask an actor to put a line into modern English that you realise how many lines are either being misunderstood or are open to interpretation. It's hardly surprising when much of the language is archaic and complex, but by going through your play line by line as a company you can be sure that everyone understands everything that is being said.

Choose a scene. Ask the actors to take their places in the space, and allocate each actor a line feeder (a little like *Shadow Play*, Game 27). The line-feeders stand at the edge of the stage and speak the actors' lines, a sentence at a time. Following the line-feed, the actor must then play the line, with all its accompanying sentiments, but in their own words. Allow them to take time doing so – and if there's a word that needs defining, stop and work out what it means. This is an active way of interrogating the text. It's possible to do this sitting round a table, but to make it an exercise where the actors play the scene on their feet is much more fun, and often helps to make sense of the action of the text.

Further, by working through the text in this way, with it being spoken in from the outside by the line-feeders, the actors have a chance to play the scene in its rawest emotional state, in their own words, with complete spontaneity as the lines are fed in. This releases them from the pressure of thinking ahead or remembering their lines.

The Aim of the Game

To ensure the actors understand the text in detail, and to find freshness and connection in every line.

Skills
Analysis, Articulation, Characterisation

Restoration and Georgian Comedy

I adore Restoration comedy, and even more so enjoy many of the Georgian plays that followed: the work of Sheridan and his female contemporaries, like Hannah Cowley and Susannah Centlivre, whose work has been all but lost since then (and is ripe for revivals, ladies and gents). But I have to confess, whilst I love the form on the page, I often don't enjoy it in the theatre. Restoration as a genre seems to have suffered from rather misguided teaching. Student productions are often played with so much falsity and melodrama, facing the front and aiming at caricatures rather than characters, that any subtlety and genuine connection is lost. And, unsurprisingly, if the texts are treated like bald pantomimes, it's very difficult for an audience to engage or relate. However, the good news is they don't have to be like that – and when they're played with sensitivity to the period style *and* with truthfulness and simplicity, then they can be wonderful.

Restoration comedies exploded onto the scene when Charles II came galumphing on to the throne in 1660. Prior to that England had been subject to a very dull period where everything was beige: the Puritans banned all forms of fun, from theatre and public singing to Christmas celebrations. So, when Charles arrived from his sojourn on the Continent and kicked the Puritans to the seventeenth-century kerb, he brought with him all things loud, bright and sexy. He reopened the theatres, commanded comedies to be written, and, after seeing it first in Paris, allowed women on the stage for the first time.

The consequence of the cultural shift from no theatre to full-throttle entertainment was that many playwrights tried desperately hard to 'entertain'. Plays were often all show and, quite literally, no trousers. With women in the companies, most of whom were prostitutes, writers held nothing back, making sure the men in the audience got their money's worth from the theatrical spectacle. They wrote breeches parts for the women, in which women dressed as men, thereby revealing their shapely legs to the audience. Most plays of this type culminated in the 'reveal scene' in which the woman was exposed as a women through her breasts being bared or some other shocking act. And, as if that wasn't enough, the men in the audience could pay an extra penny to watch the actresses change backstage.

This isn't to suggest that the early Restoration comedies were all lewd. Many writers like Aphra Behn and William Wycherley were true comic writers. However, there was certainly a trend for vulgarity. Sexual puns and themes were running high and the theatre became the realm of titillation. Characters were broad and often, as they were 'stock characters' inspired by Commedia dell'Arte and other European trends, they became exaggerated two-dimensional versions of reality. There was also a noticeable lack of morality in some of the populist comedies; characters chasing each other and getting their own way in love and marriage, often at the expense of others. The great writers, however, cut through this and wrote brilliantly entertaining plays which amplified the comic form, whilst also satirising the political state and tugging the heartstrings simultaneously. Quite an achievement for a generation who'd grown up with little access to theatre.

As time went on, writers began to tire of the lewdness of the early comedies. As the end of the century approached, many writers turned their backs on smut, and instead became swept up in the growing fad for sentimentalism. 'Feeling' became fashionable. Young men took to recording their emotional experiences in notebooks then, in the evenings, heading to their specially built garden grottos to practise weeping. And social activities reflected the same preoccupations. The orphanage at Coram Fields was the place to be seen, at which visitors would weep heartily (as long as people were watching) before returning to their privileged lives. And if the queues were too long at Coram, then Bedlam (Bethlem Hospital for lunatics) was a popular second choice for day trips, where you could choose between sobbing with pity or, alternatively, you could pay a penny for a stick and poke the mad people to see what they would do.

The fashion for sentimentalism extended into writing. The poetic man became the love interest, and words were used as currency in love. However, it wasn't long before astute writers saw the phoney side, and began to poke fun at the notion of the 'sentimental man'. Sheridan's plays, *A School for Scandal* in particular, reveal the writer's contempt for the false hero who speaks poetic lies in order to get his own way. Whilst his Joseph Surface is a 'man of sentiment' who uses pretty words to wile his wicked ways, his honest brother Charles, the man of feeling, rises up as the hero by the end of the play.

Sheridan and the writers of the 1700s employed both the slicing wit of the Restoration and the heart of a time when lewdness was on the decline and sentiment had been replaced by true feeling. These plays have depth and the characters have rich, fully formed personalities. If you only read one play of this period then there are few as brilliant as *The Rivals*, which I would happily argue is a near-perfect play.

In terms of character, Restoration comedies are most commonly peopled by stock characters. Often featuring a rake, a young cad (Sir Harry Wildair in George Farquhar's *The Constant Couple*), the angry cuckold (*Pinchwife* in Molière's *School for Wives*), the fop (the aptly named Sir Fopling Flutter in George Etherege's *Man of Mode*) and the witty couple who rebel against society to get their own way (Lydia Languish and Jack Absolute in Sheridan's *The Rivals*). Playwrights tended to give the characters names which hint at their behaviour. Who indeed would trust Mr Pinchwife, or want to spend the evening with Sir Jealous? And what do you think characterises a young maid called Pert? Restoration is not the realm of subtlety.

The exercises in this section introduce the comic tropes of both Restoration and Georgian plays, whilst also emphasising the need to root the characters in reality. The comedies tend to have the following features:

- The plays were performed with a heightened awareness of the audience, on an apron stage, which extended out into the auditorium. This allowed the actors to play elements of the scene directly to the audience, both in allocated asides and through a constant awareness of the audience during the scenes.

- The plays are packed full of eloquent exchanges of wit, razor sharp in both the comic repartee and the barbed social commentary.

- Thematically, plays of this period often focus on marriage for love or money, social class and questions of morality, often in relation to honesty versus secrecy, or sentiment versus feeling.

In *Pick Me!* we investigate the actor-audience relationship. *Tea for Three* goes one step further and looks at the specific placement of asides and how to find a balance between onstage action and repartee with a present audience. In *Pinchwife and Sons* we look at the naming of characters and have some fun creating various creatures from the stock repertoire. In *Marry Your Daughters* we investigate the reality of the marriage market, the Restoration's most popular theme, and explore what defines a 'good prospect' when you are spouse-hunting. Finally, *Lady Frizzle's Feather* looks at the nature of gossip and scandal in the plays.

Pick Me!

A quick-fire game to get actors to play to the audience.

How to Play

Anyone who's ever been to a comedy at an open-air theatre, Shakespeare's Globe or Regent's Park, for example, will know that a great deal of the hilarity comes from interaction with the audience. This doesn't just mean the actors sending lines out to a sea of faces, but picking individuals to speak to, to heighten the humour of a line.

We know Restoration comedy was audience-embracing because it is full of asides. An aside is a line spoken specifically and covertly to the audience, rather than to the other actors onstage – and Sheridan is the true master of the art. (Shakespeare used asides too, which may well have inspired these later writers.) Have a look at Act Three, Scene Three of *The Rivals*, in which Jack Absolute is caught in a predicament. His lover's guardian, Mrs Malaprop, shows him an insulting letter about her which we know he has written. She doesn't. Throughout the scene, Jack directs lines to the audience to share his dilemma with us: how can he maintain the deception? The comedy of the scene comes from the contrast between the lines he speaks to her, attempting to maintain a polite façade, and to us, in which we see his panic.

An inexperienced actor might stick very strictly to the asides: giving them out to the audience, but playing the rest of the scene to Mrs Malaprop. An experienced actor, in contrast, will bring the audience in from the outset, so that they feel they are truly part of the scene. He will also, most likely, share more of the lines with the audience than are prescribed as asides, in order to find extra comedy in the situation. However, it takes practice to get this technique right. Here is one way to tackle it.

Ask the actors to play the Restoration scene. The rest of the company are the audience. They can raise their hand above their heads, as if to say: 'Pick me!' Now, as the scene plays out, the actor's aim is to make sure there are no hands in the air. When an audience member gets a look or address from one of the actors, they put their hand down, until such a time as they want attention again. The actors must both play the scene and try to keep their audience satisfied.

This exercise is particularly effective when rehearsing speeches to the audience as it encourages the actor to speak directly to specific audience members, rather than simply sending the text out in the vague direction of the onlookers. They should look for opportunities to make lines specific to an audience member. Is their line a complaint about 'young men today'? If so, the actor should pick a young man to blame for those woes. If it's a flirtatious line, flirt with an audience member. This interaction can be a great deal of fun and is one of the principal reasons I enjoy directing these plays.

The great Sir Donald Sinden played asides like no other. In his preparation for playing Lord Foppington in Vanbrugh's *The Relapse* in 1969, he was given an invaluable piece of advice by Baliol Holloway. I know no one who could put it better:

> *An aside must be directed to a given seat in the theatre – a different seat for each aside, some in the stalls, some in the circle. Never to the same seat twice – the rest of the audience will think you have a friend sitting there. If you are facing to the right immediately before the aside, then direct it to the left of the theatre, and vice versa. Your head must crack round in one clean movement, look straight at the occupant of the seat, deliver the line and crack your head back to exactly where it was before. The voice you use must be different from the one you are using in the play. If loud, then soft; if soft, then loud; if high, then low; if low, then high; if fast, then slow; if slow, then fast. During an aside, no other characters must move at all – the time you take does not exist for them.*

> Donald Sinden, Laughter in the Second Act

The Aim of the Game

To increase the actors' confidence in speaking directly to the audience.

Skills
Comedy, Interaction, Observation

Tea for Three

A game in which you literally incorporate the audience.

How to Play

The audience in Restoration comedy is an ever-present part of the play. In the original performance conditions, the audience would have been partially lit, in order that the actors could address them directly. For an actor in these plays, it should feel as if, at selected points, the audience are a part of the scene.

By way of example, read Act Two, Scene One of Sheridan's *A School for Scandal*. Look at how many of Lady Teazle's lines might be played to a third character, at Sir Peter's expense.

> LADY TEAZLE: ...Though I was educated in the country, I know very well that women of fashion in London are accountable to nobody after they are married.
>
> SIR PETER: Very well, ma'am, very well; so a husband is to have no influence, no authority?
>
> LADY TEAZLE: Authority! No, to be sure: if you wanted authority over me, you should have adopted me, and not married me: I'm sure you were old enough.
>
> SIR PETER: Old enough!—ay, there it is. Well, well, Lady Teazle, though my life may be made unhappy by your temper, I'll not be ruined by your extravagance!
>
> LADY TEAZLE: My extravagance! I'm sure I'm not more extravagant than a woman of fashion ought to be.
>
> SIR PETER: No, no, madam, you shall throw away no more sums on such unmeaning luxury ... Oons! madam—if you had been born to this, I shouldn't wonder at you talking thus; but you forget what your situation was when I married you.
>
> LADY TEAZLE: No, no, I don't; 'twas a very disagreeable one, or I should never have married you.

Whilst these may not all be written as asides, it's quite clear that they are witty gags to be played at

Sir Peter's expense. Ask your actors to have a go at playing this scene (you can find the full text online). Play it once through, then, the second time, invite an extra actor to be a guest in the scene. Place them close to the actors – at the table with them, on a chair observing, sitting on the sofa next to one of the characters. Play the scene out, but this time incorporating the extra person in the conversation. If there are asides, they should be played to the guest. If there are back-handed comments, they should try to make the guest laugh. If one character is scoring points against the other, they should endeavour to get the guest on side. For Sir Peter, he may well take affront at the fact Lady Teazle is flirting with, or at least teaming up with, the guest in front of him. For Lady Teazle, this might be an opportunity to make her husband the laughing stock by ganging up on him, treating the guest as her confidante. See how this affects the scene.

Then do the same for your own Georgian or Restoration scene. You will be surprised to see how the comedy zings out as soon as you place the audience at the heart of the scene.

For a further variation, with confrontational scenes like this example between the Teazles, try dividing the audience in two on opposite sides of the stage, one group backing each character. Ask the actors to play as if they're trying to keep their team on side. They might well try and poach support from members of the other character's team. This can be a fun way to get the sparring nature of a scene to come to the fore.

The Aim of the Game

To ensure the audience has a pivotal role in the scenes, and to find specific opportunities within a scene to interact with them.

**+ Act Two, Scene One of *A School for Scandal*
by Richard Brinsley Sheridan**

Skills
Analysis, Comedy, Interaction, Rhythm

Pinchwife and Sons

An improv game to engage with the naming of characters.

How to Play

Restoration comedies are peopled with characters whose names suggest something of their habits and personalities. Writers must have enjoyed creating these dexterous puns to give their audiences clues about the characters' personalities.

There are several versions of this game. The simplest is to use names from plays which already exist. Collect names from the comedies, put each on a slip of paper and put them into a hat. Then ask the actors to take one each. One by one they must enter the space, acting as their name dictates and improvising some text. You can give them a set scenario if you wish: a job interview, or trying to hail a horse and trap, depending on how much you want to keep the exercise in the period. The audience must then guess their name. Here are some suggested names for starters:

Mr Pinchwife, Master Horner, Sir Jealous, Patch, Mrs Malaprop, Captain Absolute, Fag, Bob Acres, Lydia Languish, Sir Lucius O'Trigger, Lady Sneerwell, Sir Benjamin Backbite, Snake, Dainty Fidget, Mrs Squeamish, Sir Fopling Flutter, Medley, Mrs Loveit, Mr Smirk, Lady Townley, Pert, Busy, Marplot, Lady Ogle.

Now, for a more imaginative alternative, ask the actors to invent new Restoration character names. To give them inspiration they might use some of the following:

*   *Verbs that suggest character habits*: Poke, Whisper, Shuffle, Polish, Snigger.

*   *Nouns that suggest a personality or job*: Fox, Scabbard, Mop, Whip, Swan, Bottle.

*   *Adjectives that describe a character's behaviour*: Careless, Perfect, Wiley, Meddling, Pompous.

On slips of paper they must write the name down, and a line about what sort of character they are. Fold them up and put them in the hat, then proceed as above, with each actor pulling a name at random, acting out the character then everyone else guessing what their name might be. This can be great fun, though often pretty rude – but then what would you expect from the Restoration, where the world is peopled with characters like Pert the maid, desperate Sir George Touchwood, Lydia Languish and the meddling Marplot!

The Aim of the Game

To bring an awareness of the character types of Restoration, to get to grips with the themes and to consider the character names in your play and what they might mean.

+ Pens, paper, a hat or other container
Skills
Comedy, Improvisation, Vocabulary

Marry Your Daughters

A Restoration status game.

How to Play

Divide the ensemble into four groups – A, B, C and D. It's useful, though not essential, for Bs to be girls and Cs to be boys. Ds can be either. Then ask all the As to find a B, and Cs to find a D.

As are B's parents; Bs are A's daughters.

Cs are D's parents; Ds are C's sons.

Give everyone a playing card.

The number on the parent's card (As and Cs) dictates the wealth of their family (themselves and their sons or daughters), with 2 being the poorest and an Ace being a millionaire.

The number on the sons and daughter's card (Bs and Ds) tells you how attractive they are, with 2 being whacked by every branch of the ugly tree and Ace being off-the-scale, drop-dead gorgeous. Yes, this is a shallow game – the 1600s were shallow times.

Now, set the scene. We are at an extravagant ball. Play music if you want to. Over the course of the ball (maybe about ten minutes), the parents must set off with their children and attempt to marry them off. The daughter's parent (As) must try and marry their girl off as well as they can, to the wealthiest suitor. A woman completely relies on her fortune as she has no prospect of work at this point in history. The son's parent (Cs) must try and encourage their sons to marry classy, pretty girls. The children will obviously want to marry the most attractive option, though, of course, will hope to marry well.

You have ten minutes to introduce yourself to everyone in the room, work out your prospects, then go in for the kill. But be quick – if you are too slow the rich hotties might be snapped up before you can say "Zounds!' Wander around, show your card (subtly) to the people you are talking to, and try and make a match. If the father agrees, the son can propose. If the daughter accepts, they take a seat at the side.

Give the actors a two-minute warning so those still single can find a match before it's too late. Continue until everyone is married off, or some poor spinster is left on her own – or worse, ends up paired with the ugly mug in the corner, simply because his dad has a big estate.

The Aim of the Game

To improve improvisation skills and reinforce the theme of marriage and the manner in which it operated (this game is sadly representative of the experience of most young people in the Restoration… and, in some cases, far more recently). And to bag a match.

+ Recorded music and playing cards
Skills
Characterisation, Observation

Lady Frizzle's Feather

A Restoration gossip game.

How to Play

Almost every Restoration play relies on gossip being passed from servant to mistress, round the houses and back. For an example, look at the ensemble scenes in Sheridan's *The School for Scandal*. The characters congregate simply to pass scurrilous gossip – hardly a surprise with names like Lady Sneerwell and Benjamin Backbite.

Now it's your turn. Ask everyone to stand in a circle. Start tapping a beat with your feet. The first player, on a beat, stage whispers 'Lady Frizzle's feather…' to their neighbour. This passes round the circle, each time spoken on the beat. See how much mileage you can get out of the gossipy tones in this simple phrase. Is the feather something scandalous? Is it seductive? Is it outrageous? Hilarious?

When the gossip has gone round once, extend the sentence by adding 'Lady Frizzle's feather had its…' and go round again, with everyone playing on the joy of the extra titbit of gossip and the anticipation of what's going to come next.

Once this phrase has done a lap, complete the line 'Lady Frizzle's feather had its top knocked off!' Maintain the rhythm of the beat as you do so, with each person speaking on a new beat to keep it rhythmic. Encourage players to share the line as if it's the most meaningful bit of gossip they've ever been party to.

Then – and this is where gets really fun – pass the gossip line around the circle again, but this time each person changes a word. So it might go round something like this:

> 'Lady Frizzle's feather had its top knocked off!'
>
> 'Lady Frizzle's fellah had his top knocked off!'
>
> 'Lady Teazle's fellah had his top knocked off!'
>
> 'Lady Teazle's fellah had his head chopped off!'
> [Etc.]

If you like, you can improvise a chorus of 'oohs' and 'aahs' in order to keep the other players involved and to make gossipy sound effects as the rumour travels round the circle. Continue until it reaches a rousing conclusion. Then stop and observe how far away your rumour is from where it began.

You can repeat the game with lines of your own gossip. Be inventive. Have fun. Split the group into different circles so each makes a separate gossip round, then put them back together to create a full-scale gossip-scape. Be ludicrous with the rumours. Characters in these plays take great joy in scandal-mongering.

The Aim of the Game

To get into the spirit of the backbiting, gossip-swilling Restoration, whilst practising some rhythm skills.

Skills

Articulation, Ensemble Work, Improvisation, Rhythm

---

*Physical Theatre and
Commedia dell'Arte*

'Physical theatre' could be loosely defined as theatre which uses the body as its primary means of telling a story. There's no doubt about it, physical theatre can be one of the most fun and imaginative genres to rehearse and perform. However, it is also one of the most demanding. Every form of physical theatre, from the early comic roots in *Commedia dell'Arte* to the work of modern companies like Frantic Assembly or Punchdrunk, demands the level of physical rigour in rehearsal which we might associate more with dance. And whilst physical theatre doesn't necessarily mean 'dance' per se, the choreography of movement is always at the heart of it.

Whether you are inspired by companies like DV8 who are very much dance-based, or companies who use physical action and movement inventively to create landscape and character – like Kneehigh or Complicite – the factor that all these companies share is the importance of action as equal to, or more important than, words.

In this section you will find a host of starting points. None of these exercises requires brilliant dance skills. Each asks only that players use their bodies actively and imaginatively. As always with storytelling, the focus is on the tale itself, but the more everyone in the company can do to prepare physically and tune their number-one tools – their bodies – the better. Make sure everyone does a good warm-up at the beginning of a physical rehearsal. Check out the first part of this book for some ideas.

Whilst some of the exercises focus on ways to use the body as a storytelling device, several of them explore the basic principles of *Commedia dell'Arte*, the genre which became popular in sixteenth-century

Italy and kick-started physical comedy across Europe. Often performed in marketplaces on makeshift stages, *Commedia* consisted of improvised scenes in which stock characters – each distinguishable by their mask, persona and gait – would get into trouble, fool one another, fawn over each other and generally cause much hilarity.

Commedia dell'Arte means 'comedy of the artisans'. As such it was distinct from the other popular form of comedy at the time, *Commedia Erudita*, or 'learned comedy', written by academics and performed by amateur actors. *Commedia* was performed strictly by professional actors, who became expert in playing their set characters. The audiences quickly grew to love the short scenes or *lazzi* (short improvised scenes), which all riffed on the form – they were short, witty and full of physical jokes.

Popular *Commedia* characters were easily identifiable and much loved. Their names vary between plays or *lazzi*, but you could spot them by their clear characteristics. Principal characters include:

- *Il Dottore*: the mean and greedy doctor, often led by his large stomach.
- *Il Capitano*: the swaggering captain, an overambitious hero.
- *Pantalone*: the rich Venetian merchant, miserly, often cuckolded, led by greed.
- *Pulcinella*: a hunchbacked old crone who chases young women, led by desire.
- *The Inamorata* (the lovers): often rich and foolish in their passionate infatuation with each other.
- *Columbina*: the lady servant, clever and often enjoying intrigue, an inspiration for the Restoration comic maids to follow.
- *Zanni*: the lowest-of-the-low servants, with a penchant for pickled walnuts.
- *Arlecchino*: an acrobatic character, a witty servant, who carries a wooden sword and wears the much-recognised, multicoloured diamond-patterned suit.

Many of these characters went on to feature in later plays and forms of comedy: Arlecchina, for example, later become the popular Harlequin of the English 'Harlequinade' comedies developed by John Rich in the eighteenth century, and hook-nosed Pulcinella was the origin of our Mr Punch, who along with his poor wife Judy has entertained generations of children on wind-swept English seafronts. *Commedia*'s influence can also be seen clearly in the exaggerated stock characters of pantomime (the dame, the baddie, the young lovers), farce and even TV comedy which relies on bold, archetypical characters (from *Blackadder* and *Father Ted* to *The Fast Show* and *The Catherine Tate Show*).

This chapter begins with *Commedia*-specific exercises. *Nosey Parkers* provides a starting point for leading with your body and encourages actors to create characters through working out their physical desires. Then, *Commedia Amplifier* invites actors to create scenes and then shift them into a *Commedia* style, in order to learn the significance of rhythm, repetition and routine in the form. If you are interested in more detail on *Commedia dell'Arte*, then Barry Grantham's fantastic books are a veritable treasure trove of information.

The rest of the chapter moves away from *Commedia* and explores other forms of physical theatre. *Annabella's Bananas* encourages players to use their bodies to tell stories through physicality and choreography. *Wrong Room* is a clowning game in which players have to create a comic moment using only their bodies. In *Dr Frankenstein*, actors get to have fun creating monsters using each other's body parts. And finally, in *James Bland*, players must use all of their new physical skills to create drama out of the least dramatic of all scenarios.

Nosey Parkers

An exercise using physical starting points to create character.

How to Play

Commedia dell'Arte characters – and the many pantomime and comic stock characters that have evolved from them – tend to have recognisable physical traits. In particular, they have strong base desires – usually for food, sex, love or money. An easy way in to physical characterisation is to relate a character's desire to their bodies, and allow that desire to dictate movement. Try this exercise.

Everyone stands in a circle. One by one the actors cross the circle, leading with a specific part of their body. They are not only leading physically with this part, but they need to imagine their motivation to move stems from there. They lead with their groins to find a mate, their noses to sniff out gossip, their bellies to find food, their hearts to find love, etc. They must think of this body part as the location of the brain, in that it makes decisions, leads the movement impulse and pulls the rest of the body along with it.

When the player reaches the centre, they pause, sense that the object of their desire is somewhere behind them, swivel round to point their body part in that direction, and move off towards it. When they reach someone else, it is that player's turn to go in.

In order to play this game successfully, ask the actors to observe how a whole body can speak of a specific desire, rather like a cartoon character. Actors should allow their chosen body part to dictate, so the rest of the body takes a moment to follow suit, rather than simply sticking out a body part and walking with it in front of them. Observe the difference, it's remarkable.

The Aim of the Game

To explore the link between body and mind in the physicalisation of stock characters.

Skills
Characterisation, Comedy, Physicality

Commedia Amplifier

The first steps to finding a Commedia *style.*

How to Play

Whilst *Commedia dell'Arte* might be considered, in some senses, to require over-the-top acting, it's far more helpful to think of it as an amplification of life, a satire. It is the physical version of *Spitting Image*; it exaggerates physical detail based on carefully observed reality in order to reveal truth.

Commedia dell'Arte is almost like dance. Actors would learn the movements of a character down to the number of steps, the movement from foot to foot, the rhythm of a walk. If a character in *Commedia* has a change of thought, they know to stop, decide, turn, then walk again, each element with an allocated number of steps and physical gestures particular to that stock character. It is like a dancified version of life. To take an example, if you dropped a banana in real life, you might just stoop to pick it up. A *Commedia* character, in contrast, would see it, pause, position the feet, bend the top of the body, retrieve the banana, lift up the top of the body in isolation, show a reaction on the face, position the body to move, then move off.

In order to explore this style of movement, try this exercise. Ask the actors to choose a simple everyday routine: someone mending a car, a librarian putting books away, a TV chef doing a cooking demonstration. Ask the actors to play the improvisation out, paying attention to the details as they do it; their movements, any repetition, gestures, pauses, rhythms. They should note every physical movement as they make it. For example:

> A librarian walks in with a book cart, takes a book from the cart, walks towards the shelf, walks along it in one direction then the other to find the right location and then places the book.

Now, ask the actors to make it *Commedia*. They repeat the scene, but this time breaking it down into individual movements, which they should exaggerate and perform in a rhythm, giving the scene a comic style. For example:

The librarian pushes the book cart in leading with her nose because she is desperate to sniff out a place for the book. She takes three steps in, then pauses, turning to acknowledge the audience cheekily, then turns back to her book cart. She bends on the first beat, picks up the book on the second, stands up straight on the third, spins on the fourth and pauses to consider the shelf on the fifth. She now takes three steps to the left, she can't see the book's place. She pauses, taps her foot on the ground five times as she thinks, then she swivels and takes three steps to the right. Her walk this time is with her knees bent to inspect the next shelf down. She stops, no success. She swivels and, with an exaggerated comic low walk she looks along the bottom shelf of books, taking three steps to the left again. Unable to find the book's place, she pauses for thought, tapping her foot on the ground five times while she thinks. She leans on the book cart, then leans too far back as the book cart begins to slide. She pulls it back and rests on it in relief. As she does, she catches sight of a spot behind her, does a double-take, spins round, and finally places the book and leaps in the air with glee.

Try and get some of these regular comedy foils into your scenes – the double-take, the pause for thought followed by a major realisation, the exaggerated walk, the pratfall, the cheeky look to the audience. The key is that the movement must all stem from truth – whilst it's funny to act big, it's always most funny when it's recognisable and connected to reality, so it strikes a chord with us.

The Aim of the Game

To gain a basic understand of the style of *Commedia* and to explore some of its most recognisable comic tropes.

Skills
Characterisation, Comedy, Physicality, Rhythm

Annabella's Bananas

A physical-theatre exercise to introduce storytelling through the body.

How to Play

In physical theatre, the body is used as a storytelling tool in a far more comprehensive way than simply to express a character's feelings. The body might become another character, an object, an item of scenery. Bodies might together be used to create a moving vehicle, an abstract expression of a feeling, a creature. Imagination is everything in physical theatre. Imagination and stretchy trousers.

Make sure the entire company are wearing clothes they can move in, then divide them into groups of four or five. They must devise a simple story which involves a journey. It must centre around one character. For example:

- Annabella gets dressed and goes on the bus to school.

- Farah sails a boat that hits a rock. There is a rescue.

- Pia and Michael go on a road trip.

- Joshua sets off on horse back to get to market.

The group now has to work together to dramatise this sequence. The only props they are allowed are their own bodies. They should start by working out what furniture they would use if they had it at their disposal. Annabella is asleep in bed… they need a bed. She then gets up and opens the door of her bedroom, goes into the bathroom for a shower, etc. The actors must work through the sequence moment by moment, casting one actor as Annabella and the others as everything else. They must be the bed, the door, the shower etc. When they have worked out how to make each object, they must devise how to move between them. They can't just drop out of one into another; they should make the transitions flow in an engaging manner.

In some ways, the simpler the story, the better. There's often more magic in watching people play out their everyday lives with the added enchantment of physical theatre, than if the story is magical to begin with.

Each group should work through their sequence, picking appropriate music if they wish, and setting their scene to the song. Specific transitions in the music should guide the movement, so the music supports and becomes essential to the piece. The scenes shouldn't contain any speaking. When all groups have finished their scenes, share them with the rest of the company.

As an alternative, you could ask each group to work on the same story. It can be fascinating to see how different the pieces will be; a simple way of demonstrating the breadth of imagination in the room.

This game is called *Annabella's Bananas* after a physical-theatre piece devised by classmates of mine at Exeter University. Of all the groups devising plays, theirs was by far the simplest story. Most of us dramatised folk tales or news stories, creating ambitious multimedia shows and open-air spectaculars. Their was the story of a regular girl, Annabella, who went on a journey to work. But of all the pieces I saw that year, theirs stuck with me the most. The inventiveness of their choreography was extraordinary. They understood how to use the body as a tool and made sure that every part of their sequence was beautifully choreographed to conjure Annabella's world. It was over a decade ago, but I'll never forget it.

The Aim of the Game

To introduce the concept of physical theatre and to encourage players to begin to use their bodies as tools of invention.

+ Recorded music
Skills
Improvisation, Physicality

Wrong Room

A simple improv comedy game.

How to Play

Ask an actor to leave the room. Whilst they are outside they must think of a character. They then re-enter and must improvise that they have just walked into the wrong room.

It is an extremely simple game, but inventive players can have a huge amount of fun sharing their character through simple comedy. Perhaps they walk in and walk straight back out. Perhaps they walk in, see everyone, then cover up their nethers as if they are naked. Perhaps they walk in as if they're an estate agent showing a house to clients then improvise as if they've walked in on a couple in bed together. Anything is possible, the delight is in the simplicity of the set-up and our witnessing the horror when the character realises they are in the wrong room.

Try and play this game with no words. If you are exploring physical theatre, and clowning specifically, it is far more effective to work in silence as it forces everyone to rely on physicality – and often the results are much funnier.

The Aim of the Game

To introduce the idea of a comic set-up and to start experimenting with simple comic improvisations.

Skills
Comedy, Improvisation, Physicality

Dr Frankenstein

A simple way to create a comic character as a pair.

How to Play

Ask everyone to get into pairs. Player One stands in neutral; they are to become the character. Player Two is the painter (or, maybe, Dr Frankenstein); they are going to 'draw' the character's facial expression on. To do so they must hold their thumb and forefinger as if holding a tiny brush a couple of inches from Player One's face. They start with the mouth, imagining that the brush has the magnetic power to pull the muscles of Player One's face into shape.

As the painter draws the mouth, the character must move their own mouth to follow the painter's illustration, thereby pulling their mouth into a new expression. The painter then draws the cheeks – perhaps raising them up or down. Then the nose; if the character has a long nose then that might pull their face forward, whilst a snub nose might make the face retreat so the head sits further back on the neck. Next, the eyes. How open or closed are they? The painter then creates the shape of the eyebrows, the position of the jaw, then draws the rest of the character's body, guiding the character all the time with the imaginary brush, as if it is a magnet, moving their body into a new shape. The painter must think about each part of the body, especially the shoulders, the hips (where is the character's weight to be?), and the position of the feet. Then when the painter is happy with their creation, they clap their hands and the character moves off into the space, maintaining and exploring their new physicality. The painter watches them move, then can call them back by clapping again to make any final edits, before setting their monster free.

The Aim of the Game

To create a detailed physical character, and in doing so to experiment with the relationship between face, body and personality.

Skills
Characterisation, Ensemble Work, Physicality

James Bland

A game to help source physical comedy from the everyday.

How to Play

This game riffs on a similar theme to *Commedia Amplifier* but focuses specifically on comedy. You may like to play the two games together in a rehearsal to investigate different styles of physical theatre.

Split the group in half, one half to act, the other to be an audience. Choose a player from the acting group to be M – or the equivalent Head of MI5 – who will set the spies on their mission.

Begin the 'video link'. M is now hooked up and ready to give the mission instructions. M must task the spies with completing the most mundane mission they can think of. It should be as far from Bond as possible – ideally something tediously simple and everyday, for example, 'Get out of bed and make yourself a bowl of cereal.'

Then turn the music on. The spies must now complete the task as if it's the most perilous activity they've ever undertaken, hence the Bond theme music. They might have to put on special clothes, use tools or gunpowder to complete the task, or perform a ludicrously dangerous stunt action in order to open the cereal box. They should let their imaginations run wild, and use physicality as much as possible to capture both the comedy and the details of the routine; the more recognisably specific the actions are, the better.

When one group has performed their task, swap over and create a new mission for the other half.

The Aim of the Game

To explore the relationship between physicality and comedy, and to gain confidence in adding comic elements in performance.

+ James Bond/*Mission Impossible*-style music
Skills
Characterisation, Comedy, Physicality, Rhythm

PHYSICAL THEATRE AND COMMEDIA DELL'ARTE

Early Modern Comedy

From the mid-1800s to well into the 1900s there was a profusion of eloquent, elegant comedies on the London stage. Early plays, like Dion Boucicault's *London Assurance* in 1841, took the Restoration model and reinvented it to tell of life in his own time. Then, as the Victorian era was drawing to a close, Oscar Wilde delighted audiences with his society comedies, alongside his essays, poems and novels, all of which critiqued contemporary life as he saw it. Around him other writers, many of whom were Irish, were using comedies both to delight audiences and to poke fun at the behaviour of Britain's social classes. George Bernard Shaw's *You Never Can Tell*, for example, is both brilliantly funny and poignant in its raising of questions about gender and class politics.

As the twentieth century came into focus, Wilde was followed by a host of talented comedians, most notably Somerset Maugham and Noël Coward, who revived the comedy of manners and whose plays have been performed regularly ever since. Coward's hits including *Present Laughter*, *Design for Living* and *Private Lives*, to name but a few. This section focuses on how to approach the witty repartee that characterises the plays of this genre.

For actors who enjoy comedy there is little as delightful as the opportunity to play the biting repartee of the Blisses in Coward's *Hay Fever* or Cecily and Gwendolen in Wilde's *The Importance of Being Earnest*. These writers were masters of the form, and what makes their plays so eminently revivable is the brilliant wit that fizzes through every line and has proved timeless for modern audiences.

Actors playing these roles need both great comic skill and the ability to connect emotionally with the heart of the characters. However, as the latter quality is covered in the chapter on modern drama, here we will focus on tackling the comedy. These comedies of manners are most often set in the upper echelons of society, and generally involve educated characters talking intellectually about clever things, and doing so at great pace. Their speed of thought is unrealistic, but that's part of the style. An actor who attempts to play Wilde's characters with the average person's speed of thought will fail before they've begun. The comedy here – and the thought processes – are deliberately heightened and must be played as such.

Ha! is a simple exercise to help actors pinpoint where the jabs lie in the repartee, and to analyse the dialogue in point-scoring terms. *Animal Habits* investigates the social groupings within this form of comedy and looks at how pack mentality often fuels the humour. *Circle of Friends* engages with the reality of these characters: who they are and what they are like behind their comic masks. *Wife Swap* is a quick-fire exercise to help actors pick up the pace in a scene and begin to explore where and how the laughs are generated. And finally, *Stream of Consciousness* asks players to start thinking about what's *not* said. Comedies of manners rely on subtext; a good deal of the time characters are presenting a façade or not saying what they really think at all. In this exercise we unpick what is really going on in order to be able to make the most of the comedy.

Ha!

A text-based game to find the comic to and fro in a scene.

How to Play

Comedy scenes often operate on a sparring level; they are a battle of wits. Plays by Oscar Wilde and Noël Coward are full of scenes where characters score social points by throwing witticisms at each other. Let's take the famous tea scene from Act Two of Wilde's *The Importance of Being Earnest* as an example, where Cecily and Gwendolen test each other's mettle by making piercing comments whilst pretending to be polite.

Either use this scene for the exercise, or substitute a scene from the play you are working on. Give each actor a different-coloured stack of Post-it notes. Now ask them to play out the scene. Every time they score a point against the other character, they stick a Post-it note on them, whilst exclaiming 'Ha!' Continue this throughout the scene. In a great comic scene, by the end of it both your actors will be poxed with Post-its. It may go something like this:

GWENDOLEN: Are there many interesting walks in the vicinity, Miss Cardew?

CECILY: Oh! yes! A great many. From the top of one of the hills quite close one can see five counties. [*Ha! Showing off.*]

GWENDOLEN: Five counties! I don't think I should like that; I hate crowds. [*Ha!*]

CECILY (*sweetly*): I suppose that is why you live in town?

GWENDOLEN: Quite a well-kept garden this is, Miss Cardew. [*Ha! How provincial.*]

CECILY: So glad you like it, Miss Fairfax.

GWENDOLEN: I had no idea there were any flowers in the country. [*Ha! Sarcasm.*]

CECILY: Oh, flowers are as common here, Miss Fairfax, as people are in London. [*Ha!*]

GWENDOLEN: Personally I cannot understand how anybody manages to exist in the country, if anybody who is anybody does. [*Ha!*] The country always bores me to death.

CECILY: Ah! This is what the newspapers call agricultural depression, is it not? [*Ha! Well read.*] I believe the aristocracy are suffering very much from it just at present. It is almost an epidemic amongst them, I have been told. [*Ha! I'm still genteel.*] May I offer you some tea, Miss Fairfax? [*Ha! I kept my cool and therefore win a social point.*]

GWENDOLEN: Thank you. [*Ha! Kept my cool too.*] (*Aside.*) Detestable girl! But I require tea!

CECILY: Sugar?

GWENDOLEN: No, thank you. Sugar is not fashionable any more. [*Ha!*]

(*Cecily puts four lumps of sugar into the cup.*) [*Ha!*]

CECILY: Cake or bread and butter? [*Ha! There's a choice – what a luxury.*]

GWENDOLEN: Bread and butter, please. Cake is rarely seen at the best houses nowadays. [*Ha!*]

CECILY (*to the Butler, cutting a large slice of cake and putting it on the tray*): Hand that to Miss Fairfax. [*Ha! Look, I have a servant to bend to my whim.*]

GWENDOLEN: You have filled my tea with lumps of sugar, and though I asked most distinctly for bread and butter, you have given me cake. I am known for the gentleness of my disposition, and the extraordinary sweetness of my nature, [*Ha!*] but I warn you, Miss Cardew, you may go too far.

CECILY: To save my poor, innocent, trusting boy from the machinations of any other girl there are no lengths to which I would not go. [*Ha!*]

Over the course of this scene Cecily scored 9 and Gwendolen 7 (though she could easily get some more if she plays the nuances of the lines). The girls are relatively evenly matched and the balance is pretty even throughout. In other scenes you will often find one character holds all the power for half of the scene before a revelation knocks them for six and the other character will win a series of points all in a row. It can be a helpful way of observing the shape of a scene and balance of power, as well as simply looking for the gags.

As an alternative method you can get members of the audience to shout out 'Point!' each time a character wins a point, then mark it on a board to keep tally. Comedy tennis.

The Aim of the Game

To seek out the witticisms in a scene, observe the power shifts and find the greatest comedy mileage in the playing of it.

+ **Post-it Notes of at least two colours**
Skills
Analysis, Comedy, Pace

Animal Habits

Investigating group dynamics through animal behavioural patterns.

How to Play

We often use animals in drama as starting points for characterisation. This is easy to do; you simply ask the actors to consider what their character's animal might be and work with that physicality to inform their dynamic choices.

A more unusual approach, with comedies in particular, is to look at the habits of a group of animals and feed that into your ensemble work.

Many comic plays are about people forming alliances in order to get what they want. Consider the number of farces where characters swap identities, working together to outwit a third party. Or, indeed, most of Wilde's comedies, in which characters who dislike each other have to form an alliance in order to win their prize. As particular animals have recognisable ways of interacting as a group, it can be fascinating to consider which are comparable with the group dynamics in your play.

In order to do so, choose a scene from your play and identify the basic group dynamics. Who are the pack? Is there a leader? Is there a loner or a renegade character who tries to break away? Now choose an animal group that relates closely and try the scene, asking the actors using just a flavour of animal behaviour to underscore their performances. Keep the words from the text; only allow there to be a small hint, in movement, in behaviour, perhaps in intonation, of the chosen animal. Ask the actors to consider who their animal would be in the pack: are they the dominant male, the follower, the rebel?

Now, as the scene goes on, call numbers to direct the group to vary the degree of animality on a scale of 1 to 10: 1 being almost imperceptibly animal, 10 being totally animalistic. You can also ask particular characters to change their level if that's useful.

Here are some suggestions:

- *Honey bees* have one of the most hierarchical social structures in the animal kingdom: they rely on a 'caste' system in order to ensure the survival of the colony. Queen bees give birth all their lives, and secrete a particular pheromone which ensures all other female bees in the colony remain sterile (!). A drone's role is to impregnate the Queen bee. They neither have stingers nor pollen-collecting equipment so once they've mated with her, they die. Worker bees do all the chores, defend the colony, collect pollen, make honey.

- *Gorillas* have a recognisable hierarchy; the alpha-male gorilla is in charge; they maintain relationships; they're protective and emotions run high when danger is near. A gorilla who goes off alone may not be welcomed back. Watch *Planet of the Apes* for inspiration.

- *Hunting hounds* act without a leader but they get excited as a group, allow aggression to lead and are easily riled and energised by the whiff of a fox. Older dogs soon drop behind.

- *Sheep* are not intelligent; they follow each other with little awareness of danger. They scramble together, they have little sense of direction and they panic when they sense a threat, often splitting into smaller factions.

- *Cats* don't tend to act in groups; they're out for themselves though they pay attention to each other when it suits them.

- *Penguins* move in colonies, but within those groups they have specific pairs, they look after their babies as a couple and sometimes take their own route away from the group. They tend to swim and often feed in groups but they are often solitary when they are diving for food.

The Aim of the Game

To consider the nature of the ensemble and identify the dynamics, specifically the hierarchy and relationships within the group.

Skills
Characterisation, Imagination, Physicality

Circle of Friends

A game to explore how each character socialises with their peers.

How to Play

As a teenage girl in the 1990s, I adored the Maeve Binchy film *Circle of Friends*, which follows a group of young girls dealing with adolescence in rural Ireland. The film is full of scenes in which the friends, being of identical age and, for a while, experience, bare their souls to each other in a manner they never would to their parents or partners. As well as making the film lively and touching, this manner of sharing between friends is also the easiest possible device to allow us to get to know the characters in their real, most natural state. Good friends don't tend to put on a front for each other. And that is the inspiration for this exercise.

In many early modern comedies we meet a particular cross-section of characters – a social group consisting of family members, love interests and staff. Who's missing? The friends. These plays often reflect a world that the characters are expected to socialise in for society's sake, rather than interactions within real friendship groups. Noël Coward's *Hay Fever* is an example of just such a play, though one might argue that there's a good reason these difficult personalities don't seem to have any friends. Let's forgive them for that for now, though, and instead improvise their peer group in order to get to know them.

Consider who your characters might be friends with. In *Hay Fever*, the daughter Sorrel Bliss might be friends with girls from school. Simon Bliss might be matey with his rowing-club chums. The housemaid Clara might be friends with the ladies who work in the house next door. People are often most honest with their friends, so everyone in the company should begin by working out who their character's circle of friends might be.

Take each character one by one. Choose three or four other actors to play the character's friends. It is best to play the game making up new acquaintances who have similar life experiences to the protagonist, rather than trying to incorporate characters that appear in the play. The friends should be the same age, perhaps the same gender and social group; the character's most natural group of acquaintances. Lady Windemere (*Lady Windemere's Fan*) might have the ladies she visits for afternoon tea. Eliza Doolittle (*Pygmalion*) might have the other flowersellers at Covent Garden Market. Miss Prism (*The Importance of Being Earnest*) might socialise with the governesses that she studied with.

The improvisations shouldn't be prepared. The actors should decide on a place where the group would naturally meet, and choose an appropriate social activity: eating, cooking, playing cards, hiking. This gives the actors a context to work within. Now begin the improvisation and see where it goes. Don't let the scene rely too heavily on the character from the play; allow the improvisation to reveal what happens when they're in and out of focus, i.e. what advice they might give their friends, rather than them discussing the action of the play necessarily.

This can be a particularly useful exercise if you are working with actors who have small parts, who might need encouragement. It's an opportunity to invest as much in those small roles as in the leads, and to make sure the whole company take the time to think about all the characters equally, rather than just focusing on the principal roles.

The Aim of the Game

To discover as much as possible about all of the play's characters, in terms of their friendship groups, their exterior worlds and their attitudes.

Skills
Characterisation, Ensemble Work, Improvisation, Pace

Wife Swap

A quick-fire game to encourage actors to consider the other characters' perspectives.

How to Play

Early modern comedies almost always feature witty repartee between two characters who make every effort to outwit each other. The effective playing of these scenes requires speed, precision and an inside-out knowledge of the text.

One way of getting to grips with the quick-response nature of such scenes can be to ask the actors to have a go at playing both parts. This not only helps players to feel where the gags should fall, but allows them to hear how their lines play out, how it feels to be on the other end of the barbs, and to take responsibility for feeding in the cues.

Begin the rehearsal of a scene as you usually would, but do it with scripts in hand so the actors can easily pick up the other person's lines.

At any point in the scene, shout 'swap'. The actors must then swap places and become the other person in the scene. There are two ways of doing this. Either they swap and continue the scene from that point – this can be particularly fun if you swap at the point of a revelation in a scene, so that the same actor has to cope with first giving and then receiving the news. Or, when you shout 'Swap!', you can feed a line that the actors have to rewind to, so that they play the section again, as the other character. This is helpful in focusing specifically on the action of the scene, as opposed to thinking solely about character.

You can play this game if there are more than two characters in the scene, either by simply asking actors to play a role other than their own, or, if it's a scene for three of four, playing the game on rotation so each actor gets a chance to play each role. However, the game is most effective when played with duologues as there's far more focus on the one scenario from two perspectives.

It sounds like a simple exercise but, in addition to adding pace and helping deepen the actors' understanding of the comedy, it's interesting how often it opens up new interpretations and allows a more complex reading of the scene. It encourages both actors to become responsible for judging their actions from within and without. Furthermore, whilst actors are used to playing comedy for the laughs, by putting themselves in the other character's shoes, they may find it easier to connect emotionally. As we know, all good comedy works best when the roles are played with truthfulness and from the heart. It is also often interesting for an actor to observe how another might play their role, but with the safety of knowing there's no competition!

You might like to play this game regardless of the genre of the play you are rehearsing. I particularly like to play it with modern comedies because it always helps to quicken the pace of the repartee and to add energy to a scene. The benefits in terms of encouraging actors to think outside their own characters are universally useful.

The Aim of the Game

To achieve the ping-pong nature of verbal sparring, and to help an actor consider their character's behaviour from both an internal and external perspective.

Skills
Analysis, Imagination, Observation

Stream of Consciousness

A game to explore the subtext.

How to Play

The lines a character speaks are only ever a percentage of what they are thinking. In fact, what they say will often contradict their true thoughts. Consider in how many scenes a character is putting up a façade. Whilst this is a feature of naturalism in the regular use of subtext, it also plays a specific role in modern comedies, in which many characters present a polite front to cover the scorn they feel underneath. Scenes of false politeness abound throughout Wilde's writing and many later comic writers followed suit.

Subtext is the meaning underneath the spoken text. You can investigate it as follows: Firstly, run the scene once as normal to get it into focus, with the lines as written. For example, let's take a simple fictional exchange. Here's the opening lines of a date:

A: Hey, I like your dress.

B: Thanks. I bought it in Selfridges.

Then, go from the beginning again, but this time allow the actor to ad-lib around the written lines to say everything that comes to mind, yet still imagining that the other character can hear them. This round is about expanding on their lines to reveal their fuller thoughts, with no filter. The characters should speak *all* their thoughts. The scene might play out like this:

A: Hey, *so good to see you… oh that's…* I like your dress. *It's, yeah, nice. It's short.*

B: *Really?* Thanks; *yeah well, it's nothing really,* I bought it in Selfridges, *on Monday, the bus took an age… I almost didn't get there. I'm so pleased you like it, I was hoping you would… I, you know, was thinking what you might like and… yeah.*

Next, in a third round, allow the character to continue speaking their mind and the original text, but this time they can also speak their unvoiced thoughts: the backchatting voice, the inner monologue. The other actor must pretend he or she *cannot* hear this. It allows the actors to comment without affecting the shape of the scene. These are the thoughts that they'd never dare speak aloud. The scene might now run like this:

A: Hey. *Hmm. Wow. That dress is hideous. What was she thinking? Is it too early to leave? No, she's smiling at me, and now I'm staring at it, I have to say something.* I like your dress.

B: *Jesus. He's flirting with me already. Why have I frozen up? Right. Think.* Thanks. *Oh no – what else do I say? Quick...* I bought it in Selfridges. *No, I didn't?! Why did I say that? I bought it in Primark! I've never even been to Selfridges. Hell, I hope he likes me.*

Now ask the actors to play the scene again, speaking their unspoken thoughts – but this time the other character *can* hear them. The scene may end up, as a result of the truthful revelations, going in a new direction and abandoning the original text. That's fine. Just see where it leads!

A: Hey – wow, that dress is... *hideous.*

B: What?

A: It's – I mean, did something happen, did you have to borrow it –

B: No, I thought you'd like it. I bought it specially. Are you serious?

A: Sorry, I – I couldn't help but say, it's – it's awful.

B: Right. Well. Thanks. Actually, I have somewhere to be. Thanks for the date. I ordered champagne by the way – and I've finished the bottle 'cause you're *that* late. So you can pick up the bill.

This last version is perhaps less helpful in terms of getting to explore the scene, but it's always a bit of fun to see how characters might act when they're unchecked and unmonitored.

The Aim of the Game

To investigate the text and work out what's going on underneath the surface conversation.

Skills
Characterisation, Imagination, Improvisation

*Modern Drama
and Naturalism*

Most sections in this part of the book focus on how to achieve a particular style of performance. In this chapter we look at naturalistic acting which, in a sense, is how to perform without any noticeable style at all. It requires lack of artifice, a sense of believability, a commitment to playing the truth of a role. But does this mean no style? No acting? No! The modern style of acting we often refer to as *naturalism* is a style in its own right; it is today's trend, just as melodrama or the dance-like attitudes of the Restoration epitomised their eras. And it needs approaching with the same discipline. Furthermore, because it focuses on finding the truth in a performance, you can use these game to rehearse plays in other genres too, as, however heightened a style of acting, all acting should be founded in truth and genuine emotional connection.

Let's begin by considering the context. In the late 1800s, there was a growing dissatisfaction amongst European and Russian artists who felt like the theatre bore no relevance to their lives. Theatres were showing comedies of manners, which focused almost entirely on the upper classes, and melodramas which they viewed as false drama for entertainment's sake. These young thinkers were children of the revolution. Within their lifetimes they had witnessed massive social change with the Industrial Revolution and major wars. They were tuned into Darwin's developing Theory of Evolution, and all around them profound levels of poverty and social dissatisfaction were palpable daily realities. So they began to ask whether theatre could be turned into an instrument for reflecting the realities of life, rather than a salve to distract from it. Marx considered the arts to be a tool used by the upper classes to lull the working classes into a false sense of satisfaction. Konstantin Stanislavsky, Anton Chekhov and their peers were determined that it could be the opposite. In 1880, Émile Zola wrote an essay called *Naturalism on Stage*, which espoused the notion that theatre could and should be used to reflect real life back at its audience. Naturalism, he thought, should employ regular speech patterns, use detailed realistic sets and focus entirely on contemporary secular themes – no Gods and Monsters, no fantasy, no pastoral idylls or far-off lands, just identifiable, hardship-filled, real life. By doing so, the stage would act as a mirror to help the audience understand more about their own lives.

The terms 'naturalism' and 'realism' are often bandied about interchangeably, but they are quite distinct from each other. Realism attempts to reflect life as it really is. Naturalism, in contrast, specifically aims to interrogate the reasons for behaviour with a more scientific approach, and was inspired by Darwin. Naturalistic writers were not merely interested in showing reality – they wanted to unpick it and explain it. They aimed to reveal the harsh realities of poverty, gender inequality, class issues and sexuality. They often adopted a pessimistic tone in order to reflect real life. Plays like Ibsen's *Ghosts* or *A Doll's House*, Chekhov's *The Cherry Orchard* or Strindberg's *Miss Julie* dealt with real life, warts and all. What makes these plays so powerful is their writers' deep psychological interrogation of the characters, and the tension that arises from the lifelike situations with which we all identify.

Whilst the term 'naturalism' specifically refers to this period of work, it has since been borrowed to describe modern acting, in which actors attempt to make their performances as realistic as possible. The difficulty with this, of course, is that theatre is a medium of communication and all too often actors attempting naturalism fail to engage because they are too understated. Believability on stage doesn't mean doing nothing. Rather, it means representing life with an accurate depiction of detail. We mustn't forget that theatre requires *drama*, and what made those early exponents of naturalism brilliant was that they had the ambition to capture all the emotional highs and lows of real life.

Here lies the challenge for an actor approaching any such text. The characters are three-dimensional; they are layered, contradictory, they are as complex as you and I. So they need a great deal of work to unpick who they are and what motivates them. Then an actor can approach the rule with psychological truth. And – here's the tricky part – that performance has to be received and readable by the audience. Stanislavsky wrote that '*In the language of an actor, to know is synonymous with to feel.*' But he didn't mean only feeling internally and expecting that to be sufficient, a trap which many young actors fall into when they make the mistake of playing a stage scene at the minute level of micro-acting which only works on television. What Stanislavsky meant, of course, was that it is imperative to connect *emotionally*. An actor must understand the psychology of a character. Be rigorous. There is a vast difference between being truthful and being boring.

In this chapter we look at methods to find the truth in the text. The aim is to find ways to connect deeply with the character, and to work in detail. For this reason, I'd recommend playing these games whatever the genre of the play you are working on, as they encourage actors to key into the emotional truth of the characters.

In *On Guard* we look at how to find spontaneity in dialogue and truth in onstage relationships. *Back to Black* provides a series of methods to strip an actor's performance back to its raw elements, in order to investigate what's really going on for the character. *The Secret* provides means to throw new light on a well-learnt scene, by using some of the tropes of naturalism (the secret, the threat outside the door) to find the drama in a scenario. *Magnetics* looks at the push-pull in a scene; the interaction between the characters and what motivates them. Finally, *The Moon is Like…* encourages actors to consider their characters' lives outside the text, asking their opinions on the wider world, socially, politically and emotionally.

On Guard

A quick exercise to increase spontaneity in a scene.

How to Play

In order to find spontaneity in a well-rehearsed scene, it's often useful to throw in something from left-field to disturb the actors' rhythms. This game forces actors to abandon their usual delivery and respond specifically to the circumstances of the moment.

Set out a rectangular playing area in which to perform the scene. Now, along each of the long sides of the space, set up a doorway; two chairs with a gap between them will suffice. Cast two guards, who spend the scene patrolling the edges of the stage.

Now, send the actors in to the scene and ask them to play their text as if, at any moment, they might be caught. When a guard passes the door, the actors must stop their scene and pretend they weren't speaking. Once the guard is satisfied that nothing is going on, they can continue on patrol. Sometimes they might wait for a while, observing the actors. At other points they might pass the door at a pace or try to catch them out. However they choose to do so, it's imperative the actors are not caught speaking.

By playing the scene like this, the actors are prevented from landing comfortably into their learnt speech rhythms as they can no longer predict where they'll have to pause. You also find that something changes in their relationship. In an argumentative scene, for example, because there is now an intrinsic need to work together despite the argument, you may find an increased sense of connection. It's not unusual to make discoveries which could be worth feeding into the performance.

The Aim of the Game

To find fresh rhythms and greater spontaneity in the text.

+ Tape or chairs
Skills
Listening, Pace, Spontaneity

Back to Black

Three exercises for listening that pull everyone back to the text.

How to Play

Each of these exercises brings a slightly different focus on delivery. In each, the players cannot see each other's faces, so rather than reading facial expression, they must listen for vocal clues for tone and meaning.

Ask the company to get into scene pairs.

1. Back to Back

The pairs sit on the floor, back to back. They should be able to feel each other breathing and, when they speak, to feel the vibrations in each other's backs. Now ask them to speak the text, really listening to each other. Ask them to concentrate on both listening to and feeling the dialogue.

2. Hugging

Ask the two actors to embrace, with heads over each other's shoulders. Deliver the scene at the level of a whisper, so no one else should be able to hear. It is amazing how revealing this can be, and not only in scenes of intimacy, but also in confrontational scenes. The physical intimacy always exposes vulnerability.

3. In the Dark

Turn off the lights and try the scene again. This time all the actors have are their listening skills, no body contact at all. They should think about pace and tone, and use real-time pauses for thinking time. Encourage them to notice how, when the other person pauses, their awareness as a listener is heightened, as they have no physical signs to read.

Each of these exercises highlights different elements in communication – intimacy, detail and thought in its simplest, most physically stripped-down form. It can be a revelatory way of looking at a scene.

The Aim of the Game

To encourage a greater level of listening, awareness and genuine connection in a scene.

> **Skills**
> *Characterisation, Listening, Spontaneity*

The Secret

A game to help throw new light on an old scene.

How to Play

Choose a scene that you have rehearsed, and that everyone knows well. Now, hand one of the actors a card, on which you've written a secret. This can be:

1. *An objective*: e.g. You have a crush on X and want to seduce them.

2. *A state of being*: e.g. You are really drunk.

3. *A threat*: e.g. You're convinced that the police are about to arrive with an arrest warrant.

4. *Knowledge*: e.g. You know that X is Y's father.

Choose specific secrets that might add interest to the scene, and help the actors move forwards. If you are trying to encourage the actors to play with a greater state of tension, add threats – raise the stakes. Write that the cake on the table is poisoned, or there's a camera hidden in the room. If you are trying to find detail for actors with smaller roles, then write them each a character trait (they are anxious, or suffering mood swings), or a desire (like hunger or love). Some of these might stick.

For a bit of fun you can add silly ones. I particularly like giving a character an allergy, as it raises the stakes for the actor immediately. Perhaps the character is allergic to feet, or women, or air? The more serious choices, in contrast, can be very helpful in finding greater depth if you plan your secrets carefully. Actors love being given something to play that no one else knows about. Sometimes I do this in a regular rehearsal, just to keep everyone on their toes.

You can choose to give a secret to one actor, or to several. Alternatively, you can tell them all the same secret (especially if it's a threat) – but of course they won't know that each other knows.

The Aim of the Game

To add new life, energy and detail into familiar scenes.

+ Cards with pre-prepared secrets
Skills
Imagination, Spontaneity

Magnetics

An exercise to place the push-pull power dynamics in the foreground.

How to Play

We are always trying to have an effect on the person we're talking to, and that effect can usually be broken down into a push or a pull – like a magnet. In that sense, every line of spoken text could be seen as an attempt either to bring the character you are addressing towards you or push them away. In this exercise we attempt to pinpoint the effect that characters have on each other at this most fundamental level.

Choose two actors who are in a scene together. Both must take each other's right hand, like in a handshake.

Begin the scene. Now, on each line, the speaker needs to make a move – either to pull their partner gently towards them, or push them away, to hold them at arm's length. There are all sorts of variations on this; there's a vast difference between pulling someone close in and pulling them almost imperceptibly towards you, but on each line there needs to be a movement of sorts… even if a character is stalling or playing for time, it will always have a positive or negative spin.

Ask the rest of the company to observe. You can try it a couple of times to vary the strength of the dynamics. What you will probably find is that, though the scale of the drama may change, the pattern of push/pull is pretty set. When you find an exception to this rule it can give the text an interesting spin.

The Aim of the Game

To identify the dynamics in the text and play clear objectives, which reveal the effect characters are trying to have on one another.

Skills
Analysis, Characterisation, Listening

The Moon is Like…

A descriptive game to get into a character's shoes and soul.

How to Play

This is a very simple exercise, and can easily be played as an extension of *In the River Thames* (Game 63), in which actors make up stories to expand their character.

Everyone stands in a circle. One player begins. They say: 'The Moon is like…' and then finish the simile with their character's perspective of the Moon. Rather than just choosing an interesting simile, the point is that they answer in a way which expresses their character's attitude to the Moon, and through it, the universe. If they are a pessimist they may answer: 'The Moon is like a mote of dust in a vast expanse of nothing.' An optimist might reply: 'The Moon is a bright button.' A philosopher: 'The Moon is the dot of a question mark asking why are we here?'

The Moon is a good place to start as it represents their view on the Universe. For other interesting start points, try: 'God is like…', 'The Earth is like…', 'Bread is like…', 'Music is like…', 'Children are like…' Pick subjects which illuminate a bigger idea.

For a variation you might like to try 'Nora is like…' – picking characters from your play to encourage the group to nail down how they feel about each other.

You can also pick subjects specific to your play's theme. 'The rich are like…', 'Marriage is like…', 'Trades unions are like…', 'Betrayal is like…' This can help your actors work out their attitudes to events in the play, whether they are directly involved in those scenes or not.

You can also play with all the senses – for example, 'Bread smells like… / Tastes like… / Feels like… / Sounds like…' – to encourage actors to think about the way in which their character interacts with the world. Whilst some might not think in particularly literary terms, if you ask them to describe a taste or a smell they might discover something of their physical relationship with the world. A farmer, whilst he's not well-read, might describe the smell or feel of bread in a manner which shows his earthy connection to working with his hands on the land.

Ask each actor to consider the manner in which they answer as a further way to investigate their character's attitudes. Are they philosophical, or practical and straight to the point? Are they optimistic? Are they angry even to be asked?

This game is particularly useful when rehearsing naturalistic plays because it encourages investigation of a character's psychology, but it is so much fun – and often so illuminating – that I tend to play it in every rehearsal process, regardless of the genre of the text.

The Aim of the Game

To explore characters' viewpoints and traits, and discover the way in which they sensorily relate to the world.

Skills
Characterisation, Imagination

New Plays

There are few things I enjoy as much as rehearsing a new play for the very first time. If you're lucky enough to be doing so, then you can relish the fact that you and everyone else in the rehearsal room are all essential pieces of the jigsaw. Your work in rehearsals may shape characters, refigure scenes and ultimately transform the play from scratches on the page in to a fully fledged performance. You may be lucky enough to have the writer in the room with you. If so, be conscious that they will have wrung their heart and soul moulding the characters that they're now handing over to you. Like parents dropping their children off on the first day of school, it is a terrifying time for the writer. However bluff they appear, underneath they are quaking, I guarantee it. Hours of machinations, sobbing, contorting on yoga mats or pounding the paths of the local park to sort out the syntax of the line which you're about to ask casually to cut.

Working on a new play can be the most rewarding experience, but it's also one to treat with kid gloves. Writers wear their hearts on their sleeves, and you can bet that, as you sail onto your next job, this one is going to live with them, whether they like it or not, as a defining piece of their canon of work. Tread carefully.

In this section, we look at methods for interrogating a play. Rather than focusing just on the actor, we look at the play from the outside, as if viewing a building, assessing its structural integrity, enjoying its strengths and pinpointing its vulnerabilities. In Emma Thompson's 2014 screenwriting lecture for BAFTA, she likened a good script to a water balloon, whereby you can push it and punch it and, if it's strong enough, it will not burst, no matter how you pummel it in different directions. The play must work as a story. It must be robust.

In this part, we look at methods to ensure that. We then move on to investigate characters, their arcs and the details of their personalities, to ensure that they will be as fully formed and deeply layered as possible. This isn't unique to new plays, of course, but it is vital that there is enough depth in the writing to allow your actors, and future performers, to play each character as a three-dimensional person. And if that's not present in the writing, it's impossible to layer on afterwards. It needs to be there on the page, from the beginning.

We start with *Character Graphs*, a simple method for exploring a character's journey, whilst also assessing the shape of the play as a whole. Next, *Outside the Door* asks the company to consider the action between the scenes in order to understand the world of the play. *In the River Thames* is an exercise to help actors consider their characters' thoughts and feelings outside the spoken dialogue, and to think about what motivates them socially and politically. *Beat It* considers the structure of the play by splitting it into units and looking at it in miniature. And finally, *Dear Pa* gives actors an opportunity to articulate their characters' wider circumstances and feelings.

Depending on the stage the script is at, playwrights may also find these exercises useful, before writing a final draft. They may, however, be happy with every word and expect you to perform the play as written. If so, these exercises are still just as useful, as they give the company a means for finding layers and deepening understanding throughout the text. For this reason, the exercises are useful in preparation for staging any play, not exclusively new writing.

Character Graphs

A game to investigate the shape and structure of your play.

How to Play

A helpful exercise for both actors and the playwright is to track each character's journey from start to finish. By doing so a writer can ensure that their play is structurally sound, and an actor can explore the emotional shifts in their story to find the most engaging manner of playing their 'arc'.

Every character has a trajectory of their personal ups and downs throughout the play. Tragedies like *Macbeth* are characterised by a primarily negative trajectory: a protagonist begins happy and ends up sad (or often dead). The hero falls from grace. Comedies have upwards trajectories, so the protagonist's life improves over the span of the story. Dick Whittington is a classic example of a man with an upwards trajectory: he begins as nobody and becomes somebody.

The primary trajectories (those of the lead protagonist) are most often diametrically opposed to those of the B characters; Malcolm, in *Macbeth*, for example, ends up victorious; *Dick Whittington*'s King Rat ends up out on his ear. By employing these opposite forces, the dramatic tension is amplified and the audience can engage on several emotional levels at once. If a group of characters are in an identical predicament with identical reactions throughout, then there's no drama.

Before you start working on individual characters, try, as a company, to plot the shape of the play on a big sheet of paper. Along the horizontal axis mark your scene numbers, and along the vertical axis write the numbers 1 to 10, with one being the lowest and ten being highest. Ten is when everything is going right; one represents complete destruction. Now plot the story, marking a dot for each scene to show how circumstances get better or worse as the play goes on. In simple terms, are the characters happier or more compromised?

To give a simple example, let's look at a classic romcom structure. Whilst this is principally a film genre, romcoms so often follow a recognisable structure that I find they can provide an easy way in to explore dramatic shape.

In a classic romcom, we begin with two characters who know something is lacking in their lives (it's love, whether they realise that or not). So we begin with a low number, as neither feel fulfilled (let's say 3 out of 10). Then they meet, there's a spark and life perks up (5). Their lives improve as their relationship develops (7), they fall in love (8) and one proposes to the other (9) and it appears that they're on their way to blissful happiness. Then something goes wrong. One finds out the other is not who they said they were (as in *About a Boy*), dating them for a bet (*How to Lose a Guy in Ten Days*) or the owner of the evil capitalist bookstore (*You've Got Mail*). They split up and life gets worse (5) and worse (4, 3, 2…) until they realise they've lost the love of their lives and are more miserable than when they started. They hit rock bottom (1). Then, there's a twist! Something happens to turn the tables, meaning that everything gets resolved. They rekindle their romance and live happily ever after (10). A tragedy is pretty much the opposite shape.

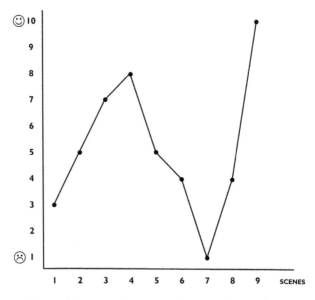

Now you've agreed on your play shape, ask each actor to plot their own character's journey on a new piece of paper. The lead character will most likely have the same shape as the play, whereas the antagonist will have the opposite. Ask them to reflect on their emotional choices across their performance and compare it to the graph. Does their way of playing the character's journey match the ups and downs appropriately? They may find they want to rethink their performance to save some of the high drama for the denouement, rather than playing too emotionally from the beginning. Max Stafford-Clark gave an excellent note whilst we were rehearsing *The Overwhelming*, a harrowing yet brilliant play about the Rwandan genocide by J.T. Rogers. It was an emotional story, but he suggested to the company that an actor must never cry more than once during a play. It is far more interesting to watch someone trying to be strong than watch them sob from the opening scene onwards. Think about it; if a friend cries occasionally you feel sorry for them; if they sob at every minor incident you will soon lose patience with them. Ask the actors to think of your audience in the same way, and save playing their strongest emotions for the most dramatic moments in the play.

Once all the actors have completed their graphs, they might like to add their trajectories to the original graph for the overall play. It will begin to look like an odd radio wave, but when you look at it as a collective emotional map you will soon see how balanced (or unbalanced) the play is. For example, if all the major events and plot points happen simultaneously, there may be benefit in peppering them throughout the story.

Whilst this game is particularly useful when developing new plays, it's also a great tool to help actors explore the shape of their emotional journeys in any text.

The Aim of the Game

To encourage actors to identify their character journeys and consider their playing choices, and to help playwrights address any structural problems.

+ Large sheets of paper and pens
Skills
Analysis, Characterisation, Ensemble Work, Structure

Outside the Door

Investigating the action between the scenes.

How to Play

When rehearsing any play, it is essential to work out what happens between the scenes. Actors must know what has happened to their character between their exits and their next entrances, in order to know their stories fully.

As a company, go through the play and make a list of the unseen action that happens between the scenes. Give each scene a simple title, e.g. 'Nell tricks Moll into eating laxatives', or 'Eddie alerts the authorities about the illegal immigrants'. Now, with all the cast sitting around the edge of the rehearsal space, work through the play from start to finish, playing the first three and last three lines of each scripted scene to 'top and tail' them, then call out the name of the 'in-between scene'. The actors must then improvise that scene. If there are multiple events between scenes, ask the actors to do minute-long versions of each scene, focusing on the key moments of offstage action. There's no need for them to play long openings into the in-between scenes; encourage them to get straight to the meaty action. Then, they must segue as seamlessly as possible into the first three lines of the next scripted scene.

You may well find you want to spend longer improvising any one of these additional scenes; if so, take the time to do so, it is always valuable work. This can be a great way to help actors create more detailed characterisations, and deepen their understanding of their circumstances. It can also be helpful for a writer to see these scenes played out, in case they choose to incorporate any of them into the final play.

The Aim of the Game

To work out the detailed journey of each character and build the backstory of offstage action.

Skills

Improvisation, Storytelling, Structure

In the River Thames

An improvisation game to explore the ways characters think.

How to Play

Everyone stands in a circle. Someone calls out a starting concept. This can be:

- *A place*: e.g. in the River Thames; on a mountain ridge; in Peckham.
- *An object*: e.g. a lemon squeezer; a shoe; a pigeon.
- *Or an idea*: e.g. Communism; the principle of free will; escape.

Each actor then must take it in turns to respond in character to a given idea, stepping forwards into the circle as they do so. To use a known play as an example, if you were rehearsing *As You Like It* and the starter concept is 'In the River Thames', the actors might respond something like this:

ROSALIND: How I would delight to swim in the River Thames and throw off my man's clothes!

ORLANDO: I once made a fleet of paper boats, bearing the name of Rosalind, and cast them into the River Thames.

TOUCHSTONE: 'Tis better to be in the River Thames, than to be 'In Seine', quoth the fool.

JACQUES: I should have drowned myself in the River Thames.

AUDREY: What's the River Thames?

You might choose to give starter concepts which relate to the theme of the play, or to explore characters' perspectives. Asking them about their religious opinions, for example, can be very revealing, as can questioning their politics and social views.

The Aim of the Game

To encourage the actors to find depth and intellectual complexity in their characterisations.

Skills
Characterisation, Imagination, Improvisation

64

Beat It

A practical exercise to help the writer work on the structure of the play.

How to Play

When developing or devising a new play, one of the trickiest elements is structure. It is hard to get perspective on this until you run the whole play, which sometimes might be too far into rehearsals – by which point it's often too late! This exercise can give you a simple means to test the structure, whilst simultaneously looking at the characters' journeys.

Firstly, split the play up into beats. A beat is a unit of action where something specific and significant happens (a Stanislavskian unit). In dialogue terms, it is where the focus shifts to a new subject. Don't make too many beats – for the purposes of the exercise it's useful to have perhaps one or two maximum per page. In other words, you are summarising your play in a little more detail than just scene by scene. Write the title of each beat on to separate pieces of paper, which should indicate, in simple terms, what happens in that section. For example, 'Megan tries to wind Frank up about his cooking' or 'Mary begs forgiveness from Elizabeth'.

Now, the cast are going to improvise the play, beat by beat, at speed. The actors should sit round the edge of the playing space, ready to jump in. Have a 'caller', who holds up each of the beat titles one by one and reads them out. As they do so, the actors in that scene get up and play the action of that beat, lasting no more than ten seconds, or the equivalent of a couple of lines from each of the key characters. The other actors, the director and the playwright should sit back and watch – and note down any point at which the action seems to jump ahead oddly, or something appears unresolved or out of place.

Once you have done this first runthrough – which should last no more than five or six minutes – lay all the beat titles out in order on the floor and talk through what worked and what didn't. Consider the possibility of moving the beats around. Don't worry about what's in which scene; from a writer's perspective, if something is wrong it has to be solved, and sometimes it's not until you see the action played out that problems become obvious.

Look at the journey of the protagonist and the way in which the action affects them. Make sure they are active throughout; plays can often be dissatisfying if things simply happen to the protagonist rather than them actively making decisions. Of course, there are examples to the contrary – Hamlet, you might say. But, in fact, he does act, and his actions propel the story forwards – it's just that the action he takes isn't the action that helps him achieve his goal.

Also check, if the play has multiple storylines, that they don't all conclude at the same point and at the same pace. As with a piece of music, good plays encompass light and shade throughout. Ensure that there is ebb and flow in the shape of the story. Whilst, of course, a play should build towards a dramatic denouement, scenes of ever-increasing pressure become predictable. Instead, characters must take their feet off the proverbial pedal occasionally, in order to surprise the audience later.

Now, if you choose to reorder the beats, repeat the improvised play and observe whether the structural changes have improved it (this is why it shouldn't last longer than five minutes). The playwright may want to rework their drama at this point in order to tell the story in a more tightly structured way.

The Aim of the Game

To explore the structure of the play and expose any problems whilst there is still time to change them.

+ Paper and pens

Skills

Analysis, Improvisation, Storytelling, Structure

Dear Pa

Improvising letters to find the character's voice.

How to Play

Letters are often used on stage as an emotional device. They are an excellent way for a character to share their internal feelings without having to speak directly to another character. In some plays, letters form the core backbone of the writing: in A.R. Gurney's *Love Letters*, for example, or Glenn Chandler's *Killers*. They are used to wonderful effect as an adjunct to the action, perhaps most memorably in Frank McGuinness's *Someone Who'll Watch Over Me*, in which the captives speak letters home out loud to share their inner thoughts. This allows them to voice fears they'd never have admitted directly to their fellow captives.

In this exercise, take these examples as your inspiration. Ask each actor to think carefully about people in their character's lives, to whom they might write. They should choose someone their character would want to share their innermost feelings with. It doesn't have to be a loved one – it could be a letter of apology, a begging letter to ask for someone's release from prison or a plea for forgiveness. The rule is it must be emotionally loaded. Actors can either spend some time writing their letters (often the most effective method) or improvise them. Sit in a circle, set out a chair for the 'reader' and listen to the letter. Consider that, in a letter, sometimes someone might be able to articulate something they could never say face to face. The letter can be an explosive means of expressing a character's most deep-rooted feelings. Sit back, listen and enjoy.

The Aim of the Game

To consider the character's inner dialogue and feelings, and, by doing so, gain a greater understanding of their actions in the play. Also, to explore relationships between characters, if the letters are addressed to other characters in the play.

Skills
Characterisation, Improvisation

PART FOUR

SOUND
AND MUSIC

*In which we create the sound and
sense of the world*

Whichever theatrical genre you are working in, finding a musical language and soundscape can be one of the most exciting elements of directing a play. Whether the music is part of the storytelling, as in a musical, or simply a way to link scenes or to underscore action, a fantastic score can illuminate a production. Likewise, working with a great sound designer can elevate your play both imaginatively and emotionally. The sound designer's job is often misunderstood; they're sometimes described as merely 'the one who does the sound effects'. But the reality is that a good sound designer will create an atmosphere that makes a play feel alive. In film and TV, the art of sound design is rightfully celebrated. 'Foley', or the making of sound effects, is a fascinating part of the drama-making process, and the innovative ways in which foley artists recreate sounds from life can be astonishing.

This section of the book encourages you to explore both the world of sound and the place of music within your production. Whilst some of the exercises encourage the company to create a soundscape, either physical or vocal, other games can be starting points for the making of songs, whilst some explore the effect of an underscore on the playing of a scene. In theatre, underscoring is often sniffed at as cheating – as if we ought to rely only on the brilliance of the actors' performances rather than music to pull on the heart strings. But there are engaging ways of employing music that don't take the focus away from the actors, but instead genuinely enhance their work. Working with a composer is one of the most delightful parts of directing, so do think about collaborating with someone whose work you find inspiring. You will not regret it.

The games in this chapter offer ways to start creating an aural language. Each can then be built on if you find their method suits you as a 'way in' to the musical landscape. In *Record Player*, we look at underscoring scenes with radically different types of music to look at the relationship between song and emotion. In *Showstopper*, the actors have the chance to improvise musically in order to tell their stories. *Soundscape Orchestra* is an ensemble exercise in which the players populate the world of the play with sound. *Musical Mash-up* is a fun way of creating a hybrid between the period of the play and contemporary culture, using music as a bridge to link themes past and present. *Infectious* is a sound and listening exercise to explore the dynamics of the group and encourage the creation of ensemble sound. *Rocky and Juliet* is an improvisation game, putting the text aside for a moment to have some fun exploring the joys of song and comedy. And finally, *Foley Box* gives players the chance to score a scene with sound effects in the manner used in film and TV, but which can make for an interesting stage performance in its own right.

Record Player

An exercise in giving a scene a new musical flavour.

How to Play

Set up to run a scene from your play as usual. Now, when the first actor comes into the space they clap their hands twice, as if switching on a high-tech physically responsive music player. At this point, start to play a song of your choice. The actors must play the scene with this piece of music as their soundtrack, allowing it to inform their performance and responding as if it is having a subconscious effect on their mood. This may accentuate the subtext of the scene as you have rehearsed it, or, often more interestingly, may give it a very different spin if the music contrasts with the emotional tone.

For the simplest game play, stick with the same song for the entirety of the scene. Or you can switch to a new song every time an actor claps their hands. Alternatively, allow each actor to choose a song in advance, and play that if they clap their hands, the song switches to their song. This can often become an engaging power struggle to see who 'owns' the tone of the scene.

The Aim of the Game

To encourage the actors to try their rehearsed scenes with a range of emotional colours, and to consider the relationship between music and feeling.

+ A range of recorded music

Skills

Characterisation, Imagination, Spontaneity

SOUND AND MUSIC

Showstopper

A rapid-response singing game to musicalise your play.

How to Play

Ask the actors to play the chosen scene as usual. At any point, you (or members of the watching ensemble if you choose) can hit an imaginary buzzer, making a loud 'Waah!' noise. When this happens, whatever line has just been spoken becomes the first line of the showstopping musical-theatre song, which they must improvise on the spot. They sing alone, sharing their thoughts and feelings about what is happening in that moment in the most arresting and overtly musical-theatre style that they can. When you press the buzzer again, the actors must pick up where exactly where they left off, as if nothing happened.

Make sure you press the buzzer at points to make sure everyone in the scene is given their chance to sing. This can be particularly comic when someone has a tiny part, and then upstages everyone in their heartfelt belting song. You can also have a good deal of fun by pressing the buzzer after lines that don't give much emotional clout. To create a showstopping number from the line 'Do you take sugar?' is far more challenging (and hilarious) than a line like 'I'm seeing someone else.'

You can either use this game as a warm-up, or as a way to explore the full extent of the characters' emotions at any point in a scene.

The Aim of the Game

To investigate characters' inner thoughts through song, whilst flexing actors' improvisation skills.

Skills
Ensemble Work, Improvisation, Voice

Soundscape Orchestra

An imaginative way to locate the aural world of your scene.

SOUND AND MUSIC

How to Play

This is a simple way to form a sound backdrop for a scene. Consider the setting of the action. Is it on the heath? In a busy Georgian street? In a Victorian house in the dead of night?

Allocate one player as the conductor and place them in the centre of the circle. The conductor will bring each player in, one by one, by gesturing for them to start their sound. These sounds can be anything that contributes to the specific tonal world of the scene, so if your scene is on the heath, players might choose the sound of the wind, the owl, the rustling grass, the creaking trees, the distant chant of witches.

The conductor indicates the volume of each player by lowering or raising their hand, adding in players from round the circle as they choose, creating a soundscape from the orchestra, making the sounds swell or soften as they wish. By using both hands together they can alter the dynamics of the whole group, raising or lowering the volume, speeding up or slowing down the pace, or changing the style of playing. The conductor can also control each player individually by pointing at them and indicating a change in dynamics. The actors must watch carefully, to ensure they follow the conductor and play their role effectively as a part of this ensemble.

The Aim of the Game

To explore the sound world of the play, whether you aim to use it as a devised element of performance or simply as a rehearsal tool to investigate the environmental setting.

Skills
Imagination, Listening, Rhythm, Voice

Musical Mash-up

How to mix modern music with period pieces to create a themed mash-up.

How to Play

You will need some music dating from the period your play is set, and some contemporary pieces that link to the themes of the play. You may like to use instruments.

I love live music in plays, and have often tried to bridge the gap between a period setting and the modern resonance of the themes using music. The composer Laura Forrest-Hay and I worked on a series of period comedies together, in which we scored the plays using musical 'mash-ups'. A mash-up is simply a song which combines two existing songs. For example, in *The Belle's Stratagem*, Hannah Cowley's Georgian play about a forward-thinking woman, we were both impressed by how modern and feminist Cowley seemed in her attitudes. We asked ourselves what she would be writing if she were still writing now, and decided the contemporary equivalent was 'girl power' song lyrics. So we chose a series of 'girl power' songs – En Vogue and Spice Girls, for example – and Laura set them to Georgian tunes, which the cast sung in full period style, as if they were ballads of their time. Every night, as soon as the audience cottoned on, there were hoots of laughter and appreciation.

The joy of this form is that it allows the play's style and period to stay in tact, and yet allows you a cheeky wink towards modernity, to offer a contemporary edge and to make reference to the similarities in attitude between the characters then and their modern counterparts now. Letitia Hardy, the young girl in *The Belle's Stratagem*, would have heartily approved of En Vogue's 'women with attitude' approach. So it was great fun hearing her sing 'My Lovin' (You're Never Gonna Get It)' with the contemporary melody set in a Georgian style, and accompanied on the harpsichord.

Start by considering which modern music is most resonant with the themes of the play you are rehearsing. Does it explore love and lust? Is it about loss? Jealousy? The hero? Attitudes to men or women? There are innumerable pop songs to choose from. Now, choose a second song, from the period in which your play is set. For example, 'Won't You Charleston with Me?' from *The Boy Friend* for an early Noël Coward play, or folk tune 'Robin Adair' for an adaptation of *Persuasion* (the song was a reputed favourite of Jane Austen's). Then, as a company or with a composer, find a way to create your mash-up by combining the two songs together. The easiest way is to set the contemporary lyrics to the period song. That way you are also more likely to sustain the period sensibilities of the piece. As an alternative, you can also try playing the contemporary song in a period style, but keeping the melody the same. Or you could use the melody from the modern song and the words from the period piece, playing the modern melody in a period style, perhaps using instruments and adding features like trills and harmony as appropriate.

Once you have tried these three options, you may have a strong feeling as to which works best. If so, work on that, but if there are elements of all three that interest you, work out how to mix them together into a single mash-up medley. Learn it and use it as a warm-up. And if it's brilliant, who knows… it might even make its way into the show!

The Aim of the Game

To find a musical language for your production, whilst also exploring the modern resonances of the themes and learning something of period music.

+ Contemporary and period music
Skills
Imagination, Rhythm, Voice

Infectious

A pass-the-sound game using a human orchestra.

How to Play

Everyone stands in a circle. Begin tapping your foot to give a basic 4/4 beat. Now, choose one person to be the 'virus' (the music-maker). They walk into the circle and make a rhythm: it could be vocal or physical (like clapping, clicking or stamping). When they've repeated their rhythm a couple of times, they begin to 'infect' the others with it by nodding at them. The infected person then has to join in with the 'virus' rhythm. The virus chooses how many people to infect; it could be one or the whole group.

At any point, a new virus can take over, i.e. another player can jump into the middle and usurp the first (who returns to the circle), making a new rhythm and beginning to infect players with that. For a while, you will have two rhythms at play. Then, when the next virus jumps in, another, then another.

There are all sorts of variations to play. You can shout 'Swap!', at which point everyone must change their rhythm to something completely different, as long as it still fits in with the original beat. The trick is trying to get a seamless change from one set of rhythms into a new 'piece', with no obvious hiatus.

You can also cast another player as the 'doctor', who can 'cure' players by walking around the edge of the circle and putting a hand on the shoulder of infected players. When they do so, the player must fade out their rhythm. If the doctor leaves their hand there, the player fades to silent and is cured. Or the doctor can leave people at varying volumes in order to add different dynamics to the piece.

Adapt the exercise to fulfil your own needs. You might like to use sounds that are part of a specific world or soundscape, the sounds of a setting, for example, or emotional sounds.

The Aim of the Game

To explore the world of sound, and to work together as an ensemble.

Skills
Focus, Rhythm, Voice

Rocky and Juliet

A comic game to explore the interplay between music and scene.

How to Play

This is a fun game that doesn't directly relate to the text of the play; rather, it's a comic warm-up to use before a music call.

Collect together songs of different styles. Try and get hold of the following styles of music, and, in advance of the rehearsal, write down each genre on a separate card.

- *Cartoon music*: e.g. Benny Hill theme.
- *Classical romance*: e.g. Prokoflev's *Romeo and Juliet*.
- *Hammer Horror/haunted house*: e.g. Franz Reisenstein's *The Mummy*.
- *Wild West*: e.g. music by Ennio Morricone.
- *Space theme*: e.g. *2001: A Space Odyssey*.
- *Epic drama*: e.g. music by Wagner.
- *War movie*: e.g. *The Dam Busters* soundtrack; can include sound effect).
- *Silent movie*: e.g. scores by Neil Brand, or Charlie Chaplin soundtracks.
- *Eighties/nineties adventure movie*: e.g. music from *Rocky* or *Indiana Jones*.

Now, ask a player to pick one of the cards at random. That dictates the genre of the music and style of the scene they are to play.

Next, send two actors into the space and ask the others to suggest characters for them that fit the chosen genre. You can keep it simple, for instance: 'a sheriff' and 'a showgirl' for a Western scene. Or, for more experienced actors, you can specify more details; for instance, 'a sheriff who wants to rid the town of baddies, but has a terrible stutter' meets 'a showgirl with stage fright'.

For a further challenge, once you've chosen characters, you can ask the players to pick another card from the pile to dictate the style of the scene. Thus they will play characters from one genre in the style of another. Following the example above, our showgirl and sheriff might find themselves playing out their scene as romantic lovers, or as if in space.

The actors now improvise the scene, with the music as their underscore, until they reach a natural conclusion.

You can, of course, use this exercise with rehearsed scenes from your play for a bit of fun. It can be annoying (and sometimes illuminating) to play a Chekhov scene as a Wild West adventure, or a Shakespeare comedy like a Charlie Chaplin movie, for example. It can help free the text and encourages the actors to be playful with their interpretations.

The Aim of the Game

To find an engaging relationship between playing style and music.

+ Contrasting, genre-specific music and cards with genres written on them

Skills
Imagination, Rhythm, Voice

Foley Box

How to introduce live sound effects into a scene.

How to Play

Foley is the art of producing sound for an audio track for film, TV or radio. Foley artists expertly reproduce a vast array of sounds from life, often in innovative ways.

The art of foley isn't much used in theatre, but it can be a great addition. Begin by assembling a box of sound-making props. It can be helpful to have a microphone and amplifier so small sounds can be heard. Think about the sorts of sounds that you might need: bells and buzzers; material to swish around; pebbles, chippings, paper, plastic chips to move for broken glass or surfaces to walk on. Foley artists have lots of tricks for particular sounds. Try thwacking a stick to make a whooshing sound, hand soap and gelatin to make squidging sounds, cutting a lettuce to make bones crunching, cellophane for fire crackles, and a large staple gun for gunshots.

Choose a scene from the play you are rehearsing, or you could write a sound-heavy scene: haunted houses or outdoor scenes offer particularly rich pickings. Alternatively, allow the actors to improvise, which can be great fun.

Select two players to be foley artists and to score the scene as the actors perform it, matching their effects exactly with the actors' words and movements. If the actor is walking up creaky stairs, the sound effect must exactly match the points at which the actor's foot hits the floor. Sounds simple? It's really not. Enjoy!

The Aim of the Game

To explore the art of foley and consider ways to incorporate live sound effects into your production.

+ Objects and props to make noise with
Skills
Focus, Imagination, Listening

PART FIVE

'BEGINNERS'

In which we wait in the wings

Well done! Rehearsals are over. You've interrogated the text, explored physicality, researched the context and understood the style of the play. Actors: you feel at one with the character, your thoughts are their thoughts, they are with you every hour or every day – you almost *are* them – for heaven's sake, they won't leave you alone! So what next? Time to get on that stage!

This section is geared towards the actors' preparation for performance. The simple truth is that most actors like time alone on stage before a performance, rather than imposed company warm-ups. This time is sacred time to prepare in your own way. However, if you want some tools to help you along, then here you are.

For actors who want solo exercises, *Working the Space* provides a series of individual vocal and physical warm-ups to tune their body and voice. *The Gallery Game* is also a solo exercise, using the text to root the actors in the space and to enter the imaginative world of the story. *Speaking of Fish* is a simple group warm-up to find focus and a sense of immediacy. Use it to enable the company to tune in to each other and generate a collective feeling of energy. *Waah!* is arguably the simplest and speediest warm-up game of all time; use it to find a sense of focus and ensemble. And finally, *Warming Up the Space* is a little exercise for the last moments before you go on…

Break a proverbial leg!

Working the Space

A series of warm-ups to settle the company into the performance space.

How to Play

Use this simple series of exercises to warm up in the space and to help everyone find their connection with the entire room, from the front row to the furthest seats in the auditorium. Ask the actors to find a space on the stage. Then give them the following instructions:

- Jog on the spot, and as you do, run through the vowels which energise the lip muscles: 'Baa, maa, paa, waa, faa, vaa, zaa, shaa, chaa.'

- Jump from side to side, saying 'Pitter patter' for each pair of jumps.

- Tap yourself all over with rapid patting movements, whilst making an 'Aah' sound. Try and feel the vibration of the 'Aah' in your body as you pat yourself down. Pat down your legs, middle and the breadth of the back. End by tapping yourself on the face, using two fingers rather than the palm of your hand, in order to get the blood moving to the surface, waking yourself up.

- Gently massage your face, trying to loosen the jaw and keep the features soft. Clean your teeth with your tongue and chew some imaginary gum.

- Take an imaginary bow and arrow and fire it, saying 'Schoom!' as the arrow fires. Keep the sound sustained until your imaginary arrow hits the back wall. Make sure you aim the arrow into the far reaches of the auditorium; try and hit that spot with your voice. Make sure you fire into each different part of the space, to get used to playing to all the seats.

- Punch the air as if punching an imaginary ball, again pushing it away to the furthest points in the auditorium. Every time you punch, say 'Pow!', enunciating clearly in order to get the lip muscles working.

- Stretch up as high as you can and wiggle your body down, making the sound 'Weeh!' from high to low as your travel down towards the floor.

- Take a big breath then blow out of your mouth, loosening the lips like a horse exhaling. Keep the face soft. Exhale all the air, then repeat. Ensure you keep the shoulders and upper body relaxed.

- Have a good shake-out, from the top of the head, all the way down the body, shaking each limb as you go, getting rid of any tension.

The Aim of the Game

All these exercises are vocal and physical warm-ups; in addition, some encourage the company to begin thinking about projecting to the back of the auditorium.

Skills
Breath, Connection, Focus, Physicality, Voice

The Gallery Game

An exercise to help place speeches in the space.

How to Play

It can be tempting for actors to internalise thoughts and turn their performances inwards when moving into the performance space. Avoid this by using this simple exercise to direct thoughts out into the space. Ask the actors to pick a section of their text, a monologue ideally, or a series of lines. Now ask them to follow these instructions:

'Imagine that you are in a gallery. On each wall are pictures of the ideas in your speech – maybe photos, artefacts, portraits. As you walk around, pinpoint a specific object to spark the beginning of each line. Point at the image, as if nailing the idea, using the gesture to punctuate the phrase. Consider the rhythm and speed of your ideas as you see them. Do they arrive in quick succession, like a list? This may manifest like a series of pictures in a row, which allow you to jump swiftly from thought to thought. Or perhaps you gaze at one picture for a while whilst you unravel a tangled idea. Sometimes the pictures may provide the answers, sometimes the question. If you speak using descriptive language, visualise the images in the pictures to make the ideas tangible. Try and use the whole space, above the audience, behind you, up on the ceiling, on the floor.'

The Aim of the Game

To project thoughts clearly in to the space, and to pick up on the descriptive language of the text.

Skills
Articulation, Clarity, Physicality, Voice

Speaking of Fish

A verbal improvisation game to get the mind focused.

How to Play

This is a great improvisation exercise to get everyone thinking quickly. It can be played with the company standing still in a circle, but in preparation for a performance, you might like to ask the group to walk on the spot as they do it, in order to keep the energy fizzing.

The rules are very simple. One person begins telling a story to the rest of the group. The others must listen out for any word with a double meaning. As soon as they hear one, they can steal the story by taking over and going off in a new direction. For example:

> PLAYER ONE: So last week I went to the cinema and saw the best film – it was about a heist, it was *great*, and –

> PLAYER TWO: Ooh, speaking of '*grate*', I dropped my keys down a grate yesterday. It took me ages to fish them out –

> PLAYER THREE: Ooh, speaking of '*fish*', I went fishing yesterday and caught a whale. An actual whale!

> PLAYER FOUR: Ooh, speaking of '*wail*', our neighbour's baby wails all the time, he just won't settle down.

> PLAYER FIVE: Ooh, speaking of '*down*', my new feather duvet… [Etc.]

In order to get play up to speed, everyone must listen hard. It's amazing how many words in the English language have double meanings. You should try and keep the pace up, with players cutting in as quickly and frequently as possible. Try not to leave a poor speaker hanging for too long!

The Aim of the Game

To get the group to focus, listen and think on their feet.

Skills
Focus, Imagination, Pace

Waah!

A speedy focus game to get the group's attention.

How to Play

Everyone stands in a circle.

One person (Player One) passes the 'Waah!' across the circle by raising their clasped hands above their head and then bringing them down in a chopping motion, as if holding an axe, whilst crying 'Waah!', to point at someone else across the circle (Player Two).

Player Two must respond by immediately raising their own clasped hands high above their head in an upwards 'Waah!' movement, as if pulling an axe free of a wood block, saying 'Waah!' as they do so. Then Player Two's immediate neighbours must 'Waah!' Player Two, by making a downwards chopping movement towards Player Two whilst crying 'Waah!' Player Two then immediately brings their arms down in a 'Waah!' at someone else across the circle, Player Three. The game continues. Anyone who makes a mistake is out.

The idea is that each 'Waah!' should be fully voiced and energised, so that each time you receive and pass it on, the energy is sustained, and ideally increased.

As the group become familiar with the game they can pick up the pace. Try to sustain a quick rhythm for excellent focus.

The Aim of the Game

To increase the group's energy, focus and sense of ensemble.

Skills
Ensemble Work, Pace, Voice

Warming Up the Space

A positivity exercise for just before the show starts.

How to Play

The playwright David Eldridge does a lovely exercise in his writing workshops. Whenever someone stands to read their work, he asks the others to warm up the space by applauding, before the writer has spoken a word. It is amazing the feeling of positivity that it brings to proceedings.

So – very simply – before the performance, ask the entire company (production team and backstage crew too, if possible) to spread themselves out to fill the whole theatre, from the back of the auditorium, to the stage. Starting very quietly, begin clapping, like the patter of light rain. Now, everyone should slowly begin to move towards the stage. Allow the clapping to get louder then add your voice and cheer as if you've just seen the best performance.

Make sure everyone claps everyone else, acknowledging and applauding them as they walk on to stage. They are brilliant! You are brilliant! Everyone in this whole blooming production is brilliant! Keep the applause going. Form a ring, then all squat down, clapping near the floor, then, all together, raise the clap, up, up, until you have your arms raised over your heads. Then break the clap with a great big 'Waah!' sound – as your hands shoot up and apart. Enjoy the good will and the feeling that you've already achieved something. You have, of course. You have a play and now, after all your hard work, you are ready to share it.

The Aim of the Game

This is a lovely exercise that not only boosts the feeling of ensemble but raises everyone's spirits, allowing the company to celebrate the fact they've all worked together to create a unique, glorious production.

Now go on and enjoy it. Good luck!

Skills
Clapping your hands… not rocket science!

CROSS-REFERENCE
INDEX OF GAMES

SKILLS

NUMBERS REFER TO GAMES NOT PAGES

Analysis
5. Guess-ticulate
25. Personal Pronouns
28. Obstacle Game, The
34. King of the Parthenon
38. Stepping Stones
39. In Your Own Words
41. Tea for Three
51. Ha!
54. Wife Swap
59. Magnetics
61. Character Graphs
64. Beat It

Articulation
7. Tongue Twisters
9. Lip Tips and Tongue Ticklers
10. Shakespeare: The Musical!
11. Broadway Baby
24. One-Pound Words
37. Knotty-pated Fools
39. In Your Own Words
41. Tea for Three
51. Ha!
54. Wife Swap
59. Magnetics
61. Character Graphs
64. Beat It

Breath
10. Shakespeare: The Musical!
11. Broadway Baby
73. Working the Space

Characterisation
5. Guess-ticulate
16. Plasti-Scene
17. Up in Arms
25. Personal Pronouns
27. Shadow Play
28. Obstacle Game, The
29. Rubber Duck of Doom, The
32. Bryan Adams in a Toga
33. Mask Play
34. King of the Parthenon
39. In Your Own Words
43. Marry Your Daughters
45. Nosey Parkers

46. Commedia Amplifier
49. Dr Frankenstein
50. James Bland
52. Animal Habits
53. Circle of Friends
55. Stream of Consciousness
57. Back to Black
59. Magnetics
60. Moon is Like..., The
61. Character Graphs
63. In the River Thames
65. Dear Pa
66. Record Player
67. Showstopper

Clarity
7. Tongue Twisters
9. Lip Tips and Tongue Ticklers
24. One-Pound Words
74. Gallery Game, The

Comedy
3. Running Man
40. Pick Me!
41. Tea for Three
42. Pinchwife and Sons
45. Nosey Parkers
46. Commedia Amplifier
48. Wrong Room
50. James Bland
51. Ha!

Communication
17. Up in Arms
18. To Be or Not to Bee
33. Mask Play

Confidence
2. Jelly Beans
4. Five Rhythms

Connection
24. One-Pound Words
73. Working the Space

Ensemble Work
8. Rhythm Ball
13. Ring of Masons
15. Chair Pairs
17. Up in Arms
18. To Be or Not to Bee

ALPHABETICAL LIST

NUMBERS REFER TO GAMES NOT PAGES

NOTES

NOTES

NOTES

NOTES

NOTES

NOTES